THE RICH GET RICHER

American Wage, Wealth and Income Inequality

THE RICH GET RICHER

American Wage, Wealth and Income Inequality

Thomas Hyclak
Lehigh University, USA

 **World Scientific**

NEW JERSEY · LONDON · SINGAPORE · BEIJING · SHANGHAI · HONG KONG · TAIPEI · CHENNAI · TOKYO

Published by

World Scientific Publishing Co. Pte. Ltd.

5 Toh Tuck Link, Singapore 596224

USA office: 27 Warren Street, Suite 401-402, Hackensack, NJ 07601

UK office: 57 Shelton Street, Covent Garden, London WC2H 9HE

Library of Congress Cataloging-in-Publication Data

Names: Hyclak, Thomas, author.

Title: The rich get richer : American wage, wealth and income inequality /
    Thomas Hyclak, Lehigh University, USA.

Description: Hackensack, NJ : World Scientific, [2024] |
    Includes bibliographical references and index.

Identifiers: LCCN 2023020237 | ISBN 9789811277290 (hardcover) |
    ISBN 9789811277306 (ebook for institutions) | ISBN 9789811277313 (ebook for individuals)

Subjects: LCSH: Income distribution--United States. | Wealth--United States. | Wages--United States.

Classification: LCC HB523 .H93 2024 | DDC 339.20973--dc23/eng/20230606

LC record available at https://lccn.loc.gov/2023020237

British Library Cataloguing-in-Publication Data

A catalogue record for this book is available from the British Library.

For any available supplementary material, please visit
https://www.worldscientific.com/worldscibooks/10.1142/13438#t=suppl

Desk Editors: Logeshwaran Arumugam/Geysilla Jean

Typeset by Stallion Press
Email: enquiries@stallionpress.com

Printed in Singapore

Preface

A few years ago, a visiting relative spotted a book on inequality on my shelf, said he was really interested in learning more about that topic and asked to borrow it. A few months later, he returned it, complaining that he hadn't been able to understand much of what he'd read, even though the book had been written for a general audience. This gave me the initial thought that a volume that could clearly describe the data on wage, wealth and income inequality and summarize the economic analysis of that data might be useful. Further support for that idea came from several articles documenting how little people knew about U.S. inequality and how this had become a barrier to the development of inequality policy. So, what follows is my attempt to provide readers with such a book. My main approach is to structure the book around a number of charts, mostly depicting changes over time but sometimes showing close relationships between inequality and other variables. I know that charts are not everyone's cup of tea but I think that looking carefully at pictures of what's happened makes it easier to comprehend the magnitude of changes over time in the economic disparities among American workers and their families.

I was also attracted to this project by a long-held academic interest in issues surrounding earnings and income inequality. In fact, my first publications in influential economic journals reported on the relationship between income inequality and union contract coverage across US metropolitan areas. This was in the late 1970s when inequality was not a problem and also not a research interest of many other economists. Preparing this book has allowed me to read very recent research by a new generation of economists who have followed their interest in inequality by doing the hard work of compiling new data sets and analyzing them with new, powerful statistical methods. Most of the research I cite throughout this book are results published in the last decade or so. I hope I have been able to summarize that work in a way that makes sense to readers who are not economists.

Throughout this project, I have received considerable help from three good friends who read the drafts closely, asked excellent questions and made great suggestions for improvements. I am very grateful to Tom Pierce, Jim Stewart and Nick Fina for their time and effort on this behalf. Finally, I dedicate this book to my wife Jean. Her care has gotten me through several serious health situations in the past two years and her encouragement kept me working on this project at times when I was quite ready to abandon it.

About the Author

Thomas Hyclak is Professor Emeritus of Economics at Lehigh University. He retired in 2018 after a long tenure, during which he served as Chair of the Department of Economics and Interim Dean of the College of Business. Tom earned BA and MA degrees from Cleveland State University and holds a PhD in Economics from the University of Notre Dame. He came to Lehigh in 1979 after serving on the faculty of Ball State University for three years and enjoyed sabbatical stays at Lancaster and Cambridge Universities and a Fulbright Fellowship at the Cracow University of Economics.

Tom's wide-ranging research interests have led to numerous empirical contributions to the study of labor economics, regional economics, macroeconomics, industrial relations and human resource management. Recent papers include studies of the effect of the minimum wage on youth labor markets, the impact of English proficiency on the wages of Polish workers and the contribution of the cardiovascular revolution to economic growth. He is a co-author of *Fundamentals of Labor Economics*. Tom and his wife Jean live in Bethlehem, Pennsylvania.

Contents

List of Figures

List of Tables

Chapter 1

Introduction

A prominent feature of U.S. economic performance over the last forty years has been a steady rise in economic inequality. The spread between high and low wages has widened considerably, the ownership of wealth and the income generated by wealth have become more highly concentrated in the hands of the richest Americans and overall disparities in household income from all sources have increased, even after accounting for taxes and transfer payments from the government. While this trend toward greater inequality has also been seen in many other developed economies, the U.S. stands out for the pace at which inequality has increased, resulting in a much higher level of wage, wealth and income disparity in America.

This has attracted the attention of economists and other social scientists and a large number of empirical, theoretical and policy analyses have been added to the research literature. Public interest in this issue was slow to develop until the two big economic crises of the past decade. The Occupy Movement drew considerable attention to the wealth of the richest 1% versus the rest of us during the 2008–2010 financial crisis and great recession. Ironically, this was one of the few times in the last four decades that the share of total wealth and income going to the richest 1% of households declined slightly and temporarily. Interest in inequality also grew during 2019 and 2020 when the COVID-19 pandemic roiled the global economy. Repeated accounts of the economic and health disparities between lower-wage "essential workers" who went to work each day and those mainly high-wage individuals who were able to work from home accompanied news stories about the incidence and severity of COVID-19 infections. One tangible effect of this increased interest in inequality has been the passage of a surprising number of state referenda on minimum wage increases. However, surveys still show that people have difficulty accurately placing themselves on the income distribution ladder and have limited knowledge of how unequal U.S. incomes actually are and how fast inequality has increased.

The purpose of this book is to provide the interested reader with access to the wealth of information generated by recent research on U.S. wage, wealth and income inequality. My objective is to try to translate those research insights into terms that are clearer and easier to understand so that the reader can more fully grasp what has happened to U.S. income inequality in the years since I graduated from college. We will examine what has caused inequality to increase so dramatically over that period, what the consequences of rising inequality have been for those directly affected by economic change and for their communities and what might be done to slow the growth or reduce the level of U.S. wage, wealth and income inequality. In this introduction, I present a brief summary and guide to the topics covered and conclusions reached in the chapters to come.

1.1. The Record

Meticulous historical research, integrating a number of new sources of data, by Peter Lindert and Jeffery Williamson in *Unequal Gains: American Growth and Inequality Since 1700* has identified three distinct periods in the long-run evolution of the distribution of income over the full sweep of U.S. history. The first period was one of steadily rising household income inequality from independence to the beginning of the 20th century, punctuated only by brief periods of falling inequality in the years after the Revolutionary War and, in the South, after the Civil War. Increased inequality was driven by urbanization, industrialization and the expansion of the national and global economies and largely reflected the accumulation of wealth by the successful entrepreneurs who developed the U.S. economy. While U.S. inequality grew rapidly and reached a marked peak in the "Gilded Age" at the turn of the 20th century, income and wealth inequality in Europe was considerably higher than in America. Real wages (wages adjusted for changes in the cost of living) for unskilled laborers were significantly higher in the U.S., as evidenced by the large and steady influx of European immigrants until World War I.

During the second period, which ran from about 1910 to 1980, the long-running trend toward increased income inequality reversed course. By all measures, wages, wealth and incomes became much more equally distributed over the years from 1910 until the end of World War II and then stabilized at a low level of measured inequality until around 1980. Analysts attribute this "great leveling" to the effects of two world wars, a severe economic depression and the widespread adoption of highly progressive income and inheritance taxes on the concentration of wealth and the incomes from wealth. Pro-labor regulations and income security features of President Roosevelt's New Deal policies and wartime labor regulations were also important factors in the U.S. In addition, an important equalizing effect followed the adoption by large U.S. companies of modern human resource management methods and the creation of firm-specific "internal labor markets" that sheltered workers somewhat from labor market competition and used above-market pay rates to incentivize worker effort.

We are living in the third historical period identified by Lindert and Williamson, which has seen another reversal of course with economic inequality beginning to rise again during the late 1970s, accelerate during the 1980s and 1990s and continue to increase steadily into the first two decades of the 21st century. While inequality rose in many other advanced countries during this same period, this time the rate of increase was much faster in the U.S. and income inequality in the U.S. reached considerably higher levels than in Europe or Japan by 2020. Prominent features of this new period of rising inequality are as follows: a sharp increase in the share of total wage and salary income received by the top 1% of U.S. workers while the purchasing power of wages for those at or below the median stagnated; an increase in the amount of real and financial assets, net of debt, owned by the richest households such that the wealthiest 10% owned nearly three-quarters of all American wealth in 2020; a substantial decrease in the share of U.S. income paid to workers in wages and salaries as income from rent, interest, dividends, profits and capital gains, that is, income from the ownership of wealth, grew, and an increase in family income inequality as those earning particularly high incomes from work also increased their ownership of wealth and claims on the income from wealth.

1.2. Causes

We begin with an examination of changes in the structure of wages during the period of rising inequality since 1980. Indeed, most of this book

(Chapters 2 through 5) is focused on understanding labor market developments and their influence on the distribution of wages and salaries among American workers. This is because earnings from labor constitute the lion's share of family income for most people and because profound transformations of the U.S. labor market underlie the long rise in wage inequality. We will look primarily at the evidence for inequality effects stemming from U.S. labor market developments over the decades from 1980 to 2020. Contrasts with the period right after World War II and with developments in other high-income economies are used mainly to shed light on the U.S. situation.

By and large, economic researchers have tended to focus on the empirical or theoretical evidence for the effect of a single determinant of inequality considered in isolation from other potential causes. However, a careful reading of the evidence shows that the evolution of U.S. wage inequality over the last four decades is due to the complex interaction of several simultaneous changes in technology, globalization, labor market institutions, managerial organization and public policy in the context of recurring recessions and periods of financial instability. So, understanding the way these forces have interacted is critically important to an understanding of the current era of rising American inequality.

Economists have paid considerable attention to labor market shifts related to technological change, reflecting the rapid development and dissemination of information technology (IT) throughout the economy during the same period that wage inequality has been rising. The basic idea is neatly captured in the book titled *The Race Between Education and Technology* by Claudia Goldin and Lawrence Katz. Technological change is seen as steadily increasing the productivity and demand for skilled and more educated workers relative to those with lower levels of skill and/or educational attainment. If the supply of educated workers fails to keep up with this technology-fueled rise in demand, the wage premium for those with more education will rise as will the wage differentials between workers with different levels of educational attainment. While a rising skill-based relative wage, measured as the ratio of the wage of U.S. college graduates divided by the wage of those with just a high school diploma, can be explained by this hypothesis, the diffusion of IT has a more difficult time accounting for the observed fall in the median wage relative to that paid to the lowest wage workers since the turn of the 21st century.

A more recent avenue of research focuses on the types of tasks done by workers and machines in the production process of a firm. To date, IT has been particularly effective in automating tasks that are "routine", in the sense that each step in performing the task can be clearly delineated and written into computer code. On the other hand, IT has been less effective in automating cognitive tasks that involve judgment, analytical skills and personal interactions and in service-related tasks that require manual dexterity, flexibility and adaptability. In this way, technological change is seen as an important determinant of the "hollowing out" of the U.S. workforce, which has entailed a decrease in the share of jobs in a number of administrative support and semi-skilled production occupations held largely by workers in the middle of the overall wage distribution. As job growth has increased for high-skill and, to a lesser extent, for low-skill workers but decreased for middle-skill workers, skill-based wage differences have widened and many who formally earned "middle-class" wages have been forced to accept lower-paying jobs or drop out of the workforce.

A significant research effort has also been directed to study the effects of globalization on the distributional structure of U.S. labor income. As information and transportation costs have fallen and as policy barriers to free trade have been lowered, a marked increase in international trade, especially trade between low- and high-income countries, and in the flows of investment funds across borders coincided with much of the era of rising wage disparity. In particular, two periods stand out. During the turbulent 1970s, the post-war global monetary system, based on fixed exchange rates with the dollar, collapsed and the U.S. economy switched from being a net exporter of goods and services to becoming a net importer of goods and services. Import competition and the rise of "Japan Inc." during the decade that followed helped to accelerate the decline of U.S. manufacturing employment, especially in the Northeast and Midwest regions. Additionally, after the turn of the 21st century, globalization accelerated rapidly and contributed to another, even sharper, decline in U.S. manufacturing employment and contributed to the growing divide between skilled and unskilled workers.

Economic theory suggests that import competition from low-income countries would shift labor demand in high-income countries away from less skilled and less educated workers toward more skilled workers. Empirical evidence generally supports this hypothesis. In addition to trade competition, the reduced costs of communications and transportation and the managerial advantages of IT have also contributed to the rise of global supply chains. An oft-used example is the Apple iPhone, for which design, engineering and marketing activities are carried out by high-wage workers in the U.S. while the manufacture of components and assembly of the final product occur largely in China. Finally, IT and more open borders have allowed the off-shoring of jobs in areas like customer service and some medical diagnostics. While tradable goods and services still account for a fairly small fraction of total U.S. production, recent research has demonstrated deep and long-lasting negative effects on communities that were particularly sensitive to these types of changes in the global economy.

A third topic that has been widely studied in the wage inequality research literature is the effect of institutional changes, largely brought about by shifts in public policy and managerial practice, that also occurred during the current period of rising inequality. There is considerable evidence that the decline of union membership and collective bargaining power, partly due to the shifting industrial and geographical makeup of the U.S. economy and partly due to changes in labor law and its interpretation, has contributed to rising wage disparity. Additionally, recent research indicates that the growing industrial concentration of U.S. firms, reflecting economic factors as well as changes in the regulation of monopolies, has enhanced the labor market buying power of employers and reduced worker bargaining power over wages and employment conditions. Also adding to inequality is the managerial shift toward increased domestic subcontracting of tasks like cleaning, maintenance, security, human resources and customer service. Finally, political resistance to increasing the federal minimum wage has eroded its effectiveness in providing a floor at the low end of the wage distribution, although this has been offset to some extent by an increase in the number of states setting minimum wages above the federal level.

Thus, many dramatic changes in the American labor market over the past four decades have had the combined effect of sharply increasing the disparity in wages and salaries paid to individual workers. To consider what has happened to the distribution of family income from all sources, it is necessary to widen our focus to consider changes in the distribution of wealth and in the income derived from owning wealth, along with changes in the impact of social insurance, taxes and government transfer payments on spendable income. This is the task of Chapter 6.

Wealth refers to the ownership of real assets, like businesses or real estate, and financial assets, like stocks and bonds, net of the debts of the individual or household unit. Nonlabor income from wealth refers to the rent, profits, dividends, interest payments and capital gains received by individuals and household units. Since these payments flow from the ownership of wealth, it is common to focus attention on the distribution of wealth ownership across households. Wealth is distributed much more unequally than wage and salary income with the majority of real and financial assets owned by the richest households. At the same time, debts often outweigh much of the value of any real and financial assets owned by the majority of households.

The long-run evolution of wealth inequality in Britain, France, Germany and the U.S. is the theme of Thomas Piketty's bestselling book, *Capital in the Twenty-First Century.* His analysis of U.S. data over the decades since 1980 indicates that wealth inequality has increased dramatically as the share of national income accruing to labor has fallen and business profits and share prices have generally risen. An additional factor has been the sharp rise in the value of shares of stock used as partial compensation for highly placed business executives. The preferential tax treatment of income from financial assets and other nonlabor sources has, along with the rise of monopoly power, contributed to these gains at the top end of the wealth distribution. Additionally, the marked reduction in the progressivity of income and inheritance taxes has added to wealth inequality and to an increase in the relative importance of nonlabor income in the U.S. economy. For Piketty, the decrease in wealth inequality from 1910 to 1940, the stabilization in wealth inequality from 1940 to 1980 and the increase in wealth inequality from 1980 to the present are all primarily due to policy decisions, mainly by the federal government, and only secondarily to economic factors.

With inequality in labor earnings from wages and salaries rising steadily due to the combined forces of technology, globalization and institutional change, and inequality in the ownership of financial and real assets and the income derived from that ownership also rising over time, it should not be surprising to find that total family income from labor and nonlabor sources also became much less equally distributed over time. By 2020, the share of total income going to the richest 1% of Americans had reached levels not seen since the end of the 19th century. Spendable household income, after deducting tax payments and adding receipts from social insurance programs, like Social Security retirement and disability payments, and government transfer payments, like Medicaid and food assistance, is much more equally distributed than household labor and nonlabor earnings, or market income, in any given year. However, over the past four decades, the degree of inequality in spendable income across households has increased at about the same rate as market income inequality.

1.3. Consequences

Is it really the case that the high and steadily rising degree of income inequality experienced by the U.S. economy, taking us back to levels of disparity not seen since the end of the Gilded Age, is a serious problem that should be addressed by appropriate public policy initiatives? It is important to ask this question because inequality in and of itself is not necessarily a problem and there seems to be no objective way of defining how much inequality is too much inequality. By their nature, human beings are unequal in their physical and mental abilities. In writing *The Wealth of Nations* in 1776, Adam Smith explained how unequal wages were necessary to provide incentives for people to incur costly investments in education and training and to compensate workers for taking jobs that require higher levels of responsibility or that entail above-average risks of injury or employment instability. With regard to the level of inequality at a moment in time, almost all economists and most people, I suspect, would accept the argument that awarding high wages to those who are highly productive is "fair" and agree that the willingness of people to voluntarily accept job offers with low wages makes it difficult to characterize such offers as "unfair". Thus, we might agree that an unequal distribution of income generated by a free, competitive labor market equally open to all persons with similar levels of innate ability was fair. However, a similar conclusion would not be warranted if inequality reflected mainly gender or racial discrimination, or other obstacles to equal opportunity, in hiring and pay determination.

With regard to increases in inequality over time, an evaluation might depend on the manner in which that increase came about. A situation in which everyone's income was rising faster than the cost of living but inequality was also rising because the highest incomes increased at a slightly faster pace than the lowest incomes might not raise much concern. After all, everyone would be enjoying an increase in their material standard of living. On the other hand, it would be more troubling if inequality were rising because those at the top of the income distribution saw their incomes increasing much faster than the cost of living while the real incomes of the majority of people at the middle and bottom of the distribution stagnated or decreased over time. In fact, the latter situation has characterized much of the U.S. experience with rising inequality over the last 40 years.

So, to answer the question at the beginning of this section, an evaluation of rising inequality as a public policy problem depends largely on its causes and consequences rather than simply the question of fairness. An important factor is the role of job displacement resulting from automation, outsourcing or the decline or death of business establishments from new competition. Average workers have almost no way of diversifying the risk associated with their place of employment because the value of their skills, or human capital, becomes specific to an industry and firm with on-the-job experience and training. In addition, ownership of real estate is often the biggest component of the average worker's wealth. This means that its value is determined in the real estate market in a specific location and therefore subject to risk associated with changes in the desirability of that location. Thus, an increase in inequality occasioned by job losses in specific communities due to technological change or import competition might reflect a permanent decline in the earning power of workers living there and a decrease in their wealth due to falling home prices. If individuals are constrained in their ability to retrain because of limited resources or to move to places with greater opportunities because of weak house markets in their communities, it would be difficult to achieve a timely and efficient reallocation of resources from the point of view of society as a whole. In this case, we might argue that rising inequality was indeed a public policy problem.

Recent research has shown that communities disproportionately exposed to import competition from China after 2001 experienced population decline, a decrease in labor force participation, increased rates of disability and greater reliance on government transfer payments in addition to lower employment, wages and average house prices. In *Deaths of Despair and the Future of Capitalism*, Anne Case and Angus Deaton document a pronounced trend toward increased mortality rates from suicides, alcohol abuse and drug overdoses for U.S. men without a college education over the period since 1970. While they question the significance of a direct link to inequality, declining job opportunities and diminished wages for this group of workers appear to be the root causes of both deaths of despair and increased inequality. Such negative spillover effects on the local community and society as a whole (external costs to economists) buttress the argument for public policy to address these issues.

There are also intergenerational external costs to consider. Empirical evidence for the U.S. shows a surprisingly strong positive correlation between the rank position of a son or daughter in the distribution of income at a given age and the corresponding rank of their father or mother at the same age. Research also shows that children born during the recent rise in U.S. inequality are less likely to have earnings that surpass the earnings of their parents at the same age than children born in the immediate post-war era of low and stable inequality. In part, this is due to the importance of parental investments of time and money in the education, health and development of norms and aspirations of their children. A situation in which real income growth is stagnant or even falling for all but the highest income earners could well result in socially inefficient levels of parental investment in the human capital of their children.

Rising income inequality in the U.S. since 1980 has resulted in a markedly increased share of total income accruing to those among the top 1% of income recipients. Much attention has been paid to the disproportionate political influence this provides them given the importance of lobbying and campaign contributions in the U.S. political system. A recurring story in the media in recent years addresses how little federal income taxes, often none at all, are paid legally by American billionaires, such as Jeff Bezos and Warren Buffett. There was also reporting in 2021 and 2022 on the way private equity firms have been able to secure preferable tax treatment for their partners and on the strong resistance to President Biden's proposal to fund infrastructure investments with higher taxes on corporations and high-income individuals. A serious concern is how the ability of the rich to secure favorable tax treatment for themselves might reduce general public support for and compliance with federal tax policy.

Beyond preferential tax treatment, issues have been raised about the incentives for those with high incomes to engage in rent-seeking activity, influencing legislation and regulation to establish and protect monopoly sources of high incomes rather than investing in the competitive production of goods and services. Economists regard such behavior as having adverse consequences for economic growth as well as shifting economic power from consumers and workers to those with monopoly power. It is noteworthy that the current period of rising inequality has been associated with relatively slow growth in productivity, an increase in the extent of firm concentration and monopoly power in many industries and, more recently, a decline in the rate of new business formation.

Finally, the political power associated with high incomes means that the government may be more responsive to the policy preferences of high-income voters than to the preferences of the majority of voters whose earnings equal or fall below the median income. While this would seem to hurt the reelection chances of incumbent legislators, the ability to attract significant campaign contributions from the rich can prove to be far more important in affecting election outcomes. The political power associated with increased inequality may make it difficult to achieve an efficient allocation of resources to the production of public goods and services, such as education, health care and infrastructure, and seriously erode public confidence in the legitimacy of our system of government.

These are complicated questions that make it difficult to clearly conclude that the rise in income inequality experienced in the U.S. over the past four decades is a serious problem for society that requires public policy intervention. And evidence of adverse consequences can always be countered by arguments that inequality is required to reward merit and provide incentives to engage in beneficial economic activity. I address these issues in greater detail in Chapter 7 to provide you with a way of weighing the evidence about these problems as a prelude to a consideration of specific policy proposals.

1.4. Cures

The literature provides us with a long list of policy proposals designed to slow down the rise in U.S. inequality, if not reverse it entirely, by returning to the conditions prevailing after World War II. Before summarizing some of these proposals, it is important to take into account two aspects of the U.S. inequality experience.

First, history does not provide us with much confidence that the rise in inequality will be reduced or eliminated by the action of purely economic forces operating to restore equilibria in markets. The only period of sustained decreases in U.S. inequality occurred as the result of the combined effect of institutional and public policy innovations. One impetus came from corporate strategies to implement new systems of human resource management and internally focused pay and benefit structures designed to enhance the recruitment, selection, training and retention of workers. The administrative decisions and regulations adopted by the national labor boards during the two world wars enhanced worker bargaining power and encouraged the spread of these new human resource management systems. The sweeping legislative and regulatory New Deal policies during the Great Depression also enhanced worker bargaining rights and provided a measure of income security through minimum wages, labor regulations, unemployment insurance and social security. Finally, the need to finance wartime government spending led to the adoption of highly progressive income and inheritance tax systems. All of these factors coalesced in the institutionalization of the U.S. system of industrial relations that predominated in the first three decades following World War II.

Second, it is important to recognize how profoundly the U.S. public policy environment shifted during and after the turbulent economic and political events of the 1970s. The inability of macroeconomic policy to deal with the problems of stagflation and the rise in expectations fueled by oil price shocks; the disruption caused by the dismantling of the post-war system of international finance so soon after its creation, and the deep political divisions created by the Vietnam War, the Civil Rights Movement and President Johnson's War on Poverty fueled the rise of what has been called the "Reagan-Thatcher" revolution. This entailed widespread acceptance of the notion that government policies, labor union activities and management responsiveness to stakeholder interests rather than shareholder returns caused most economic problems and that reliance on private enterprise and free markets was the best path to increase the U.S. standard of living. This sea change in the U.S. public policy environment contributed to rising inequality in many ways and poses the important question of whether any specific inequality-reducing policy proposal can be successfully implemented in the absence of a more or less complete reversal of the policy environment.

A number of specific policy proposals to reduce inequality are directed at enhancing the earnings opportunities of those in the middle- and low-income portions of the distribution. This would include raising the minimum wage and linking it to consumer prices and changing labor law in a way that supported collective bargaining and removed the incentives to characterize workers as independent contractors or "gig" workers not covered by many provisions of labor regulations. Policy proposals to enhance the generosity of the earned income tax credit and provide child care tax credits or a universal basic income and greater health insurance subsidies would enhance the after-tax and transfer income of low-income households. The provision of universal preschool, improvements in public school education and low-tuition access to higher education would supplement parental investments in the human capital of their children. Enhanced funding for the retraining and relocation of workers displaced by import competition or technological change could accelerate the reallocation of displaced labor to its most productive use and perhaps limit the long-term negative wage and employment effects of job displacement.

Policy proposals addressed at those in the high end of the income distribution largely focus on taxes. There are arguments for reversing the post-1980 emphasis on cutting top marginal tax rates in order to bring about an increase in the progressivity of the personal income tax. This, plus taking action to limit tax loopholes that favor the rich, would lower their after-tax income and provide enhanced revenue for the redistributive and government investment policies discussed above. With regard to reducing wealth inequality, discussions have focused on implementing a direct tax on the value of assets held by wealthy individuals rather than, as in the present tax system, collecting taxes only on realized capital gains when assets are sold. In addition, the reform of inheritance tax rates and regulations has been offered as a way of limiting the inter-generational transfer and compounding of wealth inequality. Finally, a serious effort to coordinate corporate tax policy internationally could reduce the incentives of firms to account for profits in offshore tax havens and raise the revenue potential from such taxes in the countries where firms actually generate profits. Needless to say, there has been considerable political resistance to all of these tax policy proposals.

A long-term policy proposal would focus government financial support and incentives for basic research and development on IT innovations that might enhance rather than reduce employment opportunities for middle- and lower-skilled workers. Clearly, the success of such a policy would face strong headwinds as long as significant opportunities for cost reduction and profit improvement at the enterprise level continue to stem from the substitution of IT-enhanced capital and high-skill workers for other employees. However, many foresee a future in which Artificial Intelligence (AI) and machine learning, whereby computers learn to make decisions by analyzing patterns in big data, might replace large swaths of the labor force with machines that are smarter and think infinitely faster than human beings. This would appear to warrant government support for research into ways of shaping the impact of IT on the future of jobs and pay.

Even if we reach the conclusion that rising inequality should be the subject of government policy to redress its associated problems, the analysis of policy in this realm is complicated. As can be seen in the huge literature on the effects of government-supported preschool education, it can be very difficult to evaluate how effective specific interventions have been in achieving their goals. This is even more of an issue when we try to examine the potential benefits of new policy proposals. In addition, strong arguments against many proposals often turn on unintended consequences that blunt incentives for job creation and economic growth and reduce efficiency. Finally, policy is enacted through the political process which is clearly affected by the personal interest of influential people and organizations. In the second half of Chapter 7, I return to a lengthier discussion of the array of proposals offered to address inequality, the economic arguments for and against these proposals and the politics of their adoption.

1.5. Summary

High- and rising-income inequality has been a common feature of the U.S. economy for the last half-century. Fueled by technological change, the growing integration of the global economy and sweeping changes in labor market institutions and public opinion regarding income policy, this development has meant a rapidly rising standard of living for highly skilled workers and, for lengthy periods, a stagnant or falling standard of living for those filling middle- and low-skill jobs. Rising inequality has raised concerns over its adverse economic and political consequences in local communities and the nation as a whole. Greater understanding of the causes and consequences of this pervasive trend is needed to weigh the pros and cons of various policy proposals designed to counter it. I hope this brief introduction gives you a clear idea of how this book will cover the wide-ranging issues related to the topics of wage, wealth and income inequality. I also hope it has whetted your appetite for delving into the chapters to come.

Chapter 2

Concepts, Measures and Evidence
of Wage Inequality

Wage inequality refers to the distribution of compensation for time at work among individual employees. Clearly, some workers, those in minimum wage jobs, for example, earn a low hourly wage, while others, say lawyers and doctors, enjoy substantially higher hourly wages. The degree of wage inequality refers to the size of the gap between the wages of highly paid workers and those earning low wages. Changes in wage inequality over time would result from changes in demand and supply in labor markets for workers with various skills and changes in government policies and institutional forces that affect the compensation offered by employers. In this chapter, I present quite a bit of data summarized in five charts to characterize the anatomy of U.S. wage inequality, addressing such questions as follows: How has wage inequality in the U.S. changed over time? How does wage inequality in the U.S. compare with other countries? Has inequality increased even though wages rose steadily for all or have there been winners and losers? While I chart data from different sources using different inequality measures, the charts describe a consistent story about how U.S. wage inequality has changed from 1980 until today.

2.1. Measures of Inequality

The wage distribution ranks individuals by their wage level from lowest to highest and measures the fraction of individuals with earnings at each level. Except in the most unusual and likely irrelevant situations, the wage distribution will always exhibit some degree of inequality. There are always some people who earn low incomes while others earn higher incomes. In order to be able to compare two distributions and determine whether inequality is higher in one country than another or whether inequality has increased or decreased over time, we need an economical way of measuring the degree of inequality in a distribution. In general, there are two types of measures that are commonly employed and that we will encounter as we examine data or review research throughout the rest of this book. While our focus here is on measures of wage inequality, the same concepts and measures will apply when we turn our attention to the distribution of wealth and income from labor and nonlabor sources.

The first type of measure, one that is relatively easy to use, compares wage levels at different percentiles of the distribution. You might recall the concept of percentiles from standardized tests for university admissions. A score at the 90th percentile means that 90% of the test-takers had a lower score and 10% (I am rounding to whole numbers here) had a higher score. With wage inequality, it is common to compare levels at the 90th percentile with those at the 50th percentile, which is also the median, and the 10th percentile. If the difference between the 90th and 10th percentile wages is greater in economy A versus economy B, we can say that the degree of inequality is higher in A. And if the difference between the 90th and 10th percentile wages is bigger today than it was ten years ago in a given economy, we can conclude that the degree of inequality has increased over time.

We will see four variants of this approach to comparing wages at different percentiles to measure inequality in this chapter. One calculates ratios of higher percentile wages to lower percentile wages. If the earnings level denoting the 90th percentile is twice the level identifying the 10th percentile in country A but this ratio is three in country B, then B has a wider income spread and, hence, a less equal distribution. Another variant directly compares the levels and rates of change at different percentiles of the distribution. If the wage at the 90th percentile is rising at 3% a year while the 50th percentile wage is rising at 1% a year, then inequality in this economy is rising over time.

A third variant of the percentile approach examines the share of total wages earned by people falling within given percentile ranges. In recent years, a growing number of analysts describe inequality by the share of total earnings received by those in the range from the 99th to the 100th percentiles. If the share of earnings accruing to this group, which encompasses the top 1% of wage earners, is rising, then it must be the case that the share going to those in some lower percentile grouping must be falling which would indicate an increase in inequality. The final variant of the percentile comparison approach examines the average wage and salary earnings of those in various percentile ranges. How does the average earnings of those in the top 10%, the 90th to the 100th percentiles, compare with the average income of those in the bottom 10%?

Measuring inequality by comparing the earnings of workers at different percentiles is not only easy to compute and interpret but also has the advantage of permitting an examination of changes in inequality in different parts of the distribution. As we will see, this is important for the U.S. case because the changes over time between the 90th and 50th percentiles of the wage and income distributions are quite different from changes between the 50th and 10th percentiles. The disadvantage of this approach to measuring inequality is that only a few percentiles of the distribution can be readily compared, so some information about the distribution is ignored.

The second type of inequality measure attempts to avoid this disadvantage while still providing an economical index by capturing the degree of inequality of the entire distribution in a single number. One such measure is the statistical variance of wage and salary income, which measures the sum of the squared deviations of individual income levels from the mean level of income of the entire sample. The higher the variance, the greater the spread of earnings around the mean, which would indicate greater inequality among those in the sample. Another commonly used numerical index of inequality for an entire distribution is the Gini coefficient or index. The Gini coefficient measures deviations between the cumulative share of wages actually received by those in each income percentile group, ranked from the lowest to the highest, with the hypothetical share they would have received if income were equally distributed. The Gini index takes on values between zero and one, with values closer to one indicating greater inequality.

Regardless of which type of measure is employed, it is important to keep in mind two questions in order to accurately compare and contrast data and interpret research results. The first is as follows: Who is included in the sample for which inequality is being measured? How is the sample structured by gender, race, age and other characteristics? Is inequality being measured by the distribution across individuals or taxpayers or households? The second question is as follows: What income measure is being examined? Is it hourly wages or annual earnings or total household income?

2.2. An International Comparison

Information available in the online database of the Organization for Economic Cooperation and Development (OECD) allows us to put the U.S. wage inequality experience in context by comparing it with developments in Germany, Japan and the United Kingdom (U.K.). The measures of wage inequality presented in the database are percentile wage ratios, which depict wages at higher percentiles of the distribution relative to wages at lower percentiles.

In particular, we focus on three such ratios. First, inequality at the top of the distribution is described by the ratio of the wage demarking the 90th percentile of the wage distribution to the wage at the 50th percentile, or the median wage, of the distribution (the 90/50 wage ratio). To measure what happened to inequality at the low-wage end of the distribution, we focus on estimates of the ratio of the wage at the 50th percentile to the wage at the 10th percentile (the 50/10 wage ratio). Finally, the ratio of the wage at the 90th percentile relative to the 10th percentile wage (the 90/10 wage ratio) is used to place the U.S. in a ranking of a much larger number of OECD countries in 2018.

For the U.S., these ratios for the distribution of gross or before-tax, usual weekly earnings of full-time employees over 16 years of age, are available in the OECD database for each year from 1973 to 2019. The U.K. data are for the distribution of gross weekly earnings of full-time workers on adult rates of pay for each year from 1970 to 2019. Data for Japan show ratios for the distribution of gross monthly earnings of regular full-time employees for the years from 1975 to 2018. And the data for Germany measure inequality in the distribution of gross monthly earnings for full-time workers, but data are only available for the years after the reunification of East and West Germany from 1992 to 2018. Since these measures of inequality are wage ratios calculated separately for each country, the difference between weekly and monthly earnings would not matter for a comparison of whether inequality was rising and by how much. Limiting the data to the typical wages for full-time workers is of much greater importance for making cross-country comparisons.

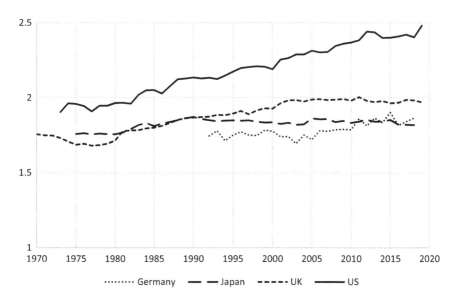

Figure 2.1:   90/50 Percentile Wage Ratios for Germany, Japan, the U.K. and the U.S.
Source: www.stats.oecd.org.

Figure 2.1 plots graphs of the 90/50 wage ratios, depicting changes over time at the top of the overall wage distributions in each of these countries over the available time periods. There are three main takeaways from the diagram, all of which help establish the conclusion that the U.S. differs considerably from these other large economies. First, top-end wage inequality, as measured by the 90/50 percentile ratio, was significantly higher in the U.S. than in any of the other countries every year. For example, in 1975, the U.S. 90/50 ratio was 15.9% higher than the U.K. 90/50 ratio and 11.4% higher than the Japanese 90/50 ratio.

Second, despite ups and downs in the U.S. 90/50 ratio in various periods, this measure of U.S. wage inequality increased at a fairly steady pace from a value of 1.97 in 1980 to a peak value of 2.48 in 2019, registering an overall rate of increase of nearly 26%. The U.K. 90/50 ratio kept pace with the U.S. measure from 1980 until 2001, but after the turn of the 21st century, the growth in U.K. top-end wage inequality essentially stopped. In Japan, top-end wage inequality increased only during the 1980s. After that decade, the 90/50 percentile ratio in Japan slowly decreased, falling by 2.6% from 1990 to 2018, a period of generally stagnant economic growth in that country. In Germany, the 90/50 ratio rose in fits and starts by 6.9% from 1992 to 2018.

Finally, by 2018, top-end wage inequality in the U.S. was substantially greater than that measured by the 90/50 wage ratios for Germany, Japan and the U.K. In 2018, the percentage difference in this measure for the U.S. and Germany was 29%; for the U.S. and Japan, it was 31.8%, and for the U.S. and the U.K., it was 21.2%. Clearly, the evolution of wages over the last half century in the U.S. labor market was much more favorable for the highest wage earners relative to those earning mid-level wages than it was in any of the other three countries examined here.

The 50/10 percentile wage ratios for each country are presented in Figure 2.2. There are some significant differences between the way this measure of inequality at the low end of the wage distribution changed over time and the results for the 90/50 ratios in Figure 2.1. First, in the mid-1970s, the U.S. 50/10 ratio was about the same as the values for the U.K. and Japan. Decreases in the ratio for those two countries meant that a gap between them and the U.S. opened up by 1980. In that year, the U.S.

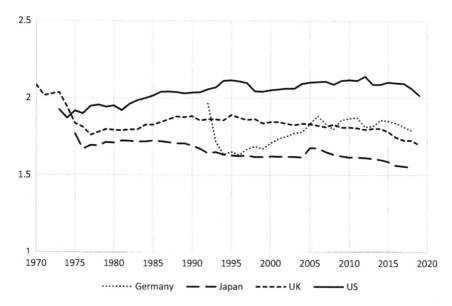

Figure 2.2:   50/10 Percentile Wage Ratios for Germany, Japan, the U.K. and the U.S.
Source: www.stats.oecd.org.

50/10 ratio exceeded the ratio in the U.K. by 8.4% and that in Japan by 13.9%.

Second, growth in the 50/10 ratio can be divided into a period of rising inequality during the decade of the 1980s and into the early 1990s followed by a period of stability or decline. The U.S. 50/10 ratio grew by 8.2%, from 1.97 in 1980 to 2.10 in 1995. After that, the U.S. ratio stayed at roughly the same level until falling a bit in 2018 and 2019. The U.K. 50/10 ratio rose by 5.6%, from 1.79 in 1980 to 1.89 in 1995, after which the trend in this measure turned slightly negative. In Japan, the 50/10 ratio was roughly constant for the early 1980s and then started a long slow decline until 2018. Finally, in Germany, the 50/10 ratio dropped sharply right after reunification and then rose steadily from about 1995 to 2006 before starting once again to fall.

Third, like with the 90/50 wage ratio, the differing movements over time in the 50/10 ratio evident in Figure 2.2 resulted in a much higher spread between mid- and low-wages in the U.S. than in the other three countries in recent years. For example, in 2018, the U.S. 50/10 ratio exceeded that of Japan by nearly 33%, was 15% higher than the German 50/10 ratio and 20% higher than the U.K. ratio. Despite distinct differences in the growth patterns for the 90/50 and 50/10 ratios, the U.S. stands out for substantially higher wage inequality by both measures in comparison with the U.K., Germany and Japan.

The U.S. also stands out for having the highest wage spread between the 90th percentile and the 10th percentile among the 37 countries in the OECD database with information available for 2018. The U.S. 90/10 percentile wage differential in that year was 4.95, indicating that workers at the 90th percentile earned a weekly wage that was almost five times the weekly wage earned by those at the 10th percentile. The other countries with 90/10 ratios above 4.0 in 2018 were Colombia at 4.73, Israel at 4.72, Costa Rica at 4.37 and Romania at 4.10. Countries with 90/10 ratios in the middle of the list were Luxembourg at 3.35, the Czech Republic at 3.34, Germany and Mexico at 3.33 and Croatia at 3.3. The lowest 90/10 percentile wage ratios in 2018 were registered by Finland at 2.58, Norway at 2.51 and Sweden at 2.14.

2.3. Gender and Race

To many, the term "wage inequality" brings to mind gender or racial/ethnic group differences in pay that might be affected by labor market discrimination. A natural question, then, is whether the increase in U.S. wage inequality is related at all to changes in gender or racial wage differentials. In general, over the period of time since 1980, the gender wage gap has narrowed somewhat (Bertrand 2020). This would have the effect of reducing wage inequality among all workers. On the other hand, the white-black wage advantage increased slightly since 1980 (Daly, Hobijn and Pedtke 2017). Here, we examine available data to compare changes over time in wage differences *between* genders and racial groups versus changes over time in wage disparity *within* gender and racial groups.

The Bureau of Labor Statistics of the U.S. Department of Labor (BLS) maintains a database that allows us to examine changes over the years from 2000 to 2020 in wage inequality between and within groups of workers identified by gender and race.[1] This database identifies the usual weekly earnings of full-time wage and salary workers over the age of 16 at various percentiles of the wage distribution for each worker group for each year from 2000 to 2020. These data are taken from the monthly Current Population Survey (CPS) which is also the source of estimates of the monthly unemployment rate and other employment and labor force information. Figure 2.3 charts these data, comparing the evolution of the wage distribution for white men and white women over the years since the turn of the 21st century. Instead of percentile wage ratios, the graph plots the real weekly wages, adjusted for inflation using the consumer price index for all urban consumers, at the 10th, 50th and 90th percentiles of the wage distributions for white men and women.

There are three takeaways from the information in Figure 2.3. First, while there is a substantial gap between male and female wages at the 50th and 90th percentiles, there doesn't appear to be any visual evidence of a significant increase in these gaps that might account for rising overall wage inequality among all workers. In fact, the female wage disadvantage at all three percentiles decreased slowly but steadily over this period, even though the lines in the graph seem to follow largely parallel tracks. For example, the median (50th percentile) inflation-adjusted weekly wage for white women was about 76% of the median wage for white men in 2000 and 82% in 2020. At the 90th percentile, the ratio of the wage for white women relative to white men grew from 71% in 2000 to 75% in 2020. Gender wage differentials narrowed over this time frame.

---

[1] See www.bls.gov/webapps/legacy/cpswktab5.htm.

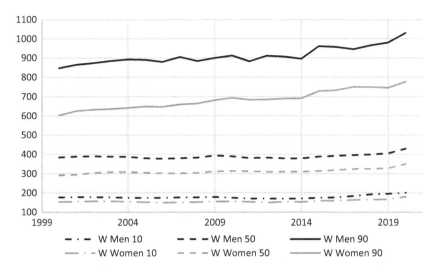

Figure 2.3: Weekly Earnings at the 10th, 50th and 90th Percentiles for White Men and Women

Source: bls.gov/webapps/legacy/cpswktab5.htm.

Second, for both men and women, the standard of living for half the population, as measured by the real purchasing power of usual weekly earnings for those at the 50th and 10th percentiles, increased very little during the first two decades of the 21st century. After 2014, there is evidence of a slight positive trend in wages at these percentiles, reflecting very low U.S. unemployment rates in the recovery from the great recession. Despite this positive development in the growth of real wages at the low end of the distribution, the rate of growth in inflation-adjusted weekly wages at the 50th percentile for the entire post-2000 period was just 11.6%, from $384 to $429, for white men and 20%, from $292 to $350, for white women. Similar to the data seen in Figure 2.1, real weekly wages at the 10th percentile grew slightly faster than the median wage from 2000 to 2020 at 13.8% for white men and 17.8% for white women.

Third, inflation-adjusted weekly wages for those at the 90th percentile did rise substantially from 2000 to 2020, with growth rates of about 22% for white men and 29% for white women. This resulted in a large increase in within-group wage inequality evident in Figure 2.3. The 90/50 percentile wage differential among white male full-time workers rose from 2.2 in 2000 to 2.4 in 2020, an increase of 9%. Among white women, the 90/50 percentile wage differential increased by 7%, from 2.07 in 2000 to 2.22 in 2020. With regard to gender wage differences, it appears that common factors causing rising wage inequality for both men and women were much more important than changes in the relative weekly wages between men and women in explaining overall wage inequality trends. The narrowing of male-female wage gaps demonstrated in Figure 2.3 would have contributed to a reduction of wage inequality among all workers.

Figure 2.4 compares changes in the distribution of weekly wages for black men and white men. Again, wages are adjusted for inflation and the graph shows weekly earnings at the 10th, 50th and 90th percentiles of the wage distributions for white and black men over the age of 16 and working full time. There is little visual evidence for a significant widening of the wage gaps between white and black men that might account for rising overall inequality since 2000. A close look reveals that the racial wage gap narrowed a bit for the highest-paid men while widening for workers at lower percentiles. Wages at the 90th percentile for black males were 70% of white males' weekly earnings in 2000 and 71% in 2020 while the

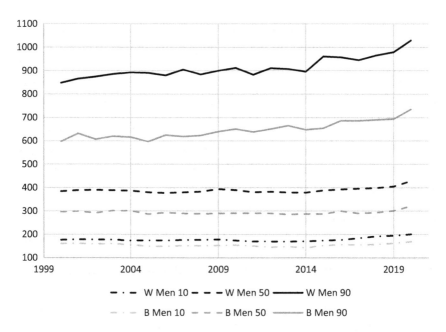

Figure 2.4:   Weekly Earnings at the 10th, 50th and 90th Percentiles for White and Black Men
Source: bls.gov/webapps/legacy/cpswktab5.htm.

median weekly wage of black men fell from 77% of the median white wage in 2000 to 75% in 2020. For those at the 10th percentile, the black-white wage ratio fell from 0.91 in 2000 to 0.84 in 2020.

Figure 2.4 provides strong visual evidence of a widening of wage inequality among both black and white men over the first two decades of the 21st century, as real weekly earnings increased most rapidly for those at the 90th percentile. As a result, from 2000 to 2020, the 90/50 percentile wage ratio rose from 2.02 to 2.3, or by 17%, for black men and from 2.2 to 2.4, or by 9%, for white men. Over the same period, the 50/10 wage ratio increased from 1.8 to 1.9, or 5.5%, for black men and fell from 2.2 to 2.1 for white men. Wage inequality increased among white men, white women and black men during the first two decades of the 21st century just as it increased for all full-time workers. However, wage inequality between white men and women and white and black men changed only slightly, in offsetting directions, over the same period. Rising U.S. wage inequality for all workers does not appear to have been driven by changes in wage differences by gender or race.

2.4. Top Wage and Salary Earners

The U.S. wage inequality estimates we have considered thus far, whether presented by the OECD or BLS, are derived from data in the monthly CPS. Such survey-based inequality measures tend to underestimate inequality in the top half of the wage distribution because of the small numbers of very high earners captured in the survey sample and because of efforts to prevent the potential disclosure of the identity of individual earners. Survey data are often top-coded, which means that the highest wage and salary earners are reported as earning at or above a certain dollar amount instead of having their actual earnings recorded. As a result, we may miss changes in the wage distribution of those whose wages are above the 90th percentile.

Researchers at the Economic Policy Institute (EPI) provide us with a way of examining the effect of including above 90th percentile earners on our conclusions about wage inequality. They use statistical methods to impute the actual earnings of top-coded workers in the CPS and estimate the wage at the 95th percentile of the distribution.[2] Figure 2.5 graphs the

---

[2]The details of their imputation and estimation methods can be found at https://www.epi. org/data/methodology and the resulting estimates are provided in the EPI State of Working America Data Library at https://www.epi.org/data/#?subject=wage-percentiles.

EPI estimates of real hourly wages at the 10th, 50th, 90th and 95th percentiles of the U.S. wage distribution from 1973 to 2020. These estimates differ from those we have seen thus far in this section in two ways. First, these are estimates of hourly wages for all employees age 16 and over who provided information on hourly wages or weekly wages and hours worked per week in the CPS. Second, the estimates are not limited to full-time employees but also include those employed part-time. This has the effect of widening the range of wages examined at both ends of the distribution. The hourly wages are expressed in dollars of 2020 purchasing power using the consumer price index for all urban consumers to adjust for price inflation.

Figure 2.5 highlights the difference in labor market outcomes between high-wage workers and those earning the median wage and below. From the graph, it appears as if the real wages at the middle and lower end of the distribution were little changed over the half-century in the chart. In fact, the 50th percentile real hourly wage grew slightly, at an average annual compound rate of just one-half of 1%, from $16.89 in 1980 to

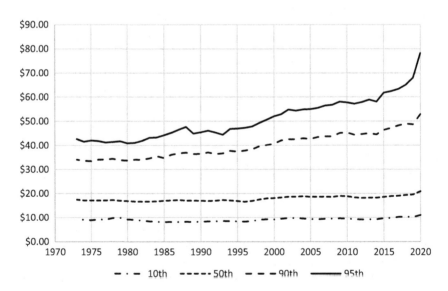

Figure 2.5: Real Hourly Earnings at the 10th, 50th, 90th and 95th Percentiles, All Workers 16 and Over

Source: Economic Policy Institute. State of Working America Data Library, Wages by Percentile and Wage Ratios, at https://www.epi.org/data/#?subject=wage-percentiles.

$20.92 in 2020. The 10th percentile real hourly wage increased by 0.4% per year, from $9.21 in 1980 to $11.01 in 2020.

By contrast, the real hourly wage received by workers at the top of the distribution increased at a much faster pace throughout the time frame and especially during the recovery from the great recession. The real hourly wage at the 90th percentile increased at an average annual compound rate of 1.1% a year, from $33.69 in 1980 to $52.88 in 2020. The real wage at the 95th percentile grew from $40.91 in 1980 to $78.72 in 2020, or at an average annual rate of 1.6%. In addition, the chart clearly shows that the growth of the 95th percentile wage outstripped that of the 90th percentile wage after 2000, even if we ignore the pandemic-influenced numbers for 2020.

As we saw in Figure 2.2, the change in wage inequality over time below the median has two different segments. The 50/10 percentile wage ratio for the data in Figure 2.5 increased from around 1.9 in the late 1970s to 2.1 in 1987 after which it fell steadily to 1.9 in 2020. Inequality above the median, on the other hand, increased considerably throughout the years depicted in Figure 2.5. The 90/50 percentile wage ratio increased from around 2 in the late 1970s to 2.5 in 2020, while the 95/50 ratio rose from 2.4 to 3.7, or by 46%, over the same time frame. The inclusion of the 95th percentile wage in Figure 2.5 also reveals a significant increase in inequality among workers earning at or above the 90th percentile. The 95/90 wage ratio increased from 1.2 in the late 1970s to 1.4 in 2020.

Including a larger proportion of high-wage workers in the sample increases our estimate of wage inequality above the midpoint of the wage distribution at any point in time but also raises our estimate of the rate of growth of wage inequality over time. The percentage change in the 95/50 ratio was 54% from the late 1970s to 2020 while the percentage change in the 90/50 ratio over the same period was less than half of that at 25%. The search for explanations of rising U.S. wage inequality in the coming chapters has to focus on the sharp difference between the real wage growth of the highest wage earners and that of workers at the midpoint of the wage distribution. In addition, explanations are needed for the changing trends, initially increasing and then declining, in the wage gap between those at the 50th and 10th percentiles.

The importance of high-wage earners in rising U.S. income inequality is also highlighted by researchers using data that are not subject to top coding. For example, Piketty (2014) concludes that most of the increase in U.S. income inequality in recent decades is due to the rise in wage and salary earnings of the highest-paid workers. Using income tax data, he estimates that the share of total wages paid out by U.S. employers going to the top 10% of wage earners increased from 25% in 1970 to 35% in 2010 while the share going to the top 1% of wage earners more than doubled from about 5% in 1970 to 11% in 2010.

Another approach, one that is often used in discussions of inequality in the media, is to compare the compensation of corporate chief executive officers (CEOs) with the pay of an average worker. CEO compensation is an element of the annual reports publicly traded corporations must file with the U.S. Securities and Exchange Commission. Mishel and Kandra's (2020) analysis of 350 large U.S. corporations found that the average CEO compensation at these firms in 2019 was $21.3 million. This figure includes the value of stock awards when vested and the value of options to buy company stock at a favorable price when those options were exercised. CEO compensation in 2019 at these firms was 320 times the average compensation (wages plus the employer's cost of benefits) of production and nonsupervisory workers in the same industry. Although the 2019 CEO wage premium was down from its peak value of 366 to 1 registered at the height of the tech stock bubble in 2000, it was still sharply higher than the 61 to 1 seen in 1989 and the 21 to 1 recorded in 1965. Trends such as these are one source of Piketty's conclusion that the rapid growth of wages paid to "super managers" (CEOs and other highly placed executives) largely accounts for the rising share of wages going to the highest U.S. wage earners. In turn, the increased share of total wages garnered by the highest earners is the major contributor to rising overall inequality.

2.5. Worker Mobility

It's also important to consider the fact that the type of data we have been examining thus far is drawn from repeated cross-section samples of the U.S. workforce. This means that each year a different set of workers makes up the sample for these inequality estimates. While the design of the survey ensures that these annual samples are representative of the entire workforce, they do not take into account the mobility of individual workers up and down the wage distribution.

Annual earnings inequality estimates can be influenced by transitory earnings, such as unusually high (or low) bonuses, temporary job losses caused by natural disasters and overtime work due to unforeseen surges in demand that would tend to be averaged out if we observed the wages of the same individuals over a longer period of time. Also, annual surveys miss the fact that workers tend to move up the wage distribution over the early and middle stages of their careers as they earn raises and promotions or switch jobs. In addition, workers move down the wage distribution as they near retirement and deal with health limitations on their productivity. If worker mobility is changing significantly over time, we might make very different inferences about trends in wage inequality from observing annual data versus data averaged over a number of years.

Researchers have drawn on data from panel or longitudinal surveys, those that interview the same group of individuals over time, to investigate the impact of worker mobility on the measurement of wage inequality. But such surveys have relatively small numbers of respondents and the number of respondents tends to diminish over time as people drop out of the survey group. An alternative approach is to construct a panel data set from the records maintained by government agencies that administer public programs. An excellent example of this approach is provided by Kopczuk, Saez and Song (2010) who use data sets developed by researchers at the U.S. Social Security Administration that combine wage information drawn from Social Security and income tax records. This gives them very large samples (1% of the entire U.S. population covered by Social Security) going back to 1937. Their main result is that wage inequality measures based on earnings averaged over 5 or 11 years for each individual follow the same trends over the period from 1980 to the mid-2000s as inequality measures based on annual earnings data. For example, the 1980 variance of earnings was around 0.5 for annual data and 0.4 for a five-year average of earnings. By 2004, inequality as measured by the variance of earnings increased at a similar pace to 0.6 for annual data and 0.5 for the five-year average earnings. The implication is that worker mobility and the incidence of transitory earnings in annual data have been quite stable over time, so annual estimates of wage inequality closely track estimates based on permanent income levels of individuals.

This conclusion is reinforced by Jäntii and Jenkins (2015) who provide a comprehensive review of the theoretical and empirical literature on worker mobility and inequality. Their reading of several studies of U.S. wage inequality leads to the conclusion that increases in long-term earnings inequality (inequality of earnings averaged over more than one year) drive increases in annual earnings inequality with changes in transitory earnings playing only a minor role. The same conclusion is reached by Bönke, Corneo and Lüthen (2015) in their study of lifetime earnings inequality in Germany and Garnero, Hijzen and Martin (2019) in their research on mobility and inequality in 24 OECD countries. While worker mobility is a potentially important factor, it turns out that none of our conclusions about the trends in U.S. wage inequality, alone or in comparison with other countries, is affected much by our reliance on measures drawn from annual survey data.

2.6. Summary

This review of data from different sources and using different measures helps identify four key characteristics of the rise in wage inequality experienced in the U.S. over the past 40 years. These will shape our discussion of the causes and consequences of rising inequality in the chapters to come and our consideration of possible cures.

1. The U.S. has much higher wage inequality than other countries belonging to the OECD and wage inequality in the U.S. grew faster over time than in Germany, Japan or the U.K. Large and rising wage disparity between workers is a rather unique characteristic of U.S. economic performance over the last half-century.
2. A main driver of rising wage inequality has been rapid growth in the wages and salaries of those at or above the 90th percentile of the U.S. distribution. The 90/50 percentile wage ratios we have examined all indicate substantial growth in the disparity between high-wage workers and workers at the middle of the wage distribution. In addition, inequality increased markedly among wage and salary recipients above the 90th percentile as the wages of the very highest earners increased the fastest.
3. By contrast, real wages of workers at the middle and lower end of the U.S. wage distribution have grown at a much slower pace. Inequality at the bottom of the distribution, as measured by the 50/10 wage ratio, increased a bit during the 1980s and the first half of the 1990s and then fell slightly from 2000 until 2020. Relatively stagnant real wages for the majority of workers at or below the median is a second driver of rising inequality. The behavior over time of the U.S. 50/10 ratio is similar to that seen in Germany, Japan and the U.K. but the level of

the American 50/10 wage ratio exceeds that found for these countries in every year since 1975.

4. Since the turn of the 21st century, the white male-white female wage gap narrowed, the white male-black male wage gap widened a bit for low-wage workers but narrowed for the highest paid, and wage inequality increased considerably among white men, white women and black men. Common factors leading to rising wage inequality among workers in each of these groups appear more important than changes in wage differentials between these groups in explaining rising wage inequality in general.

Chapter 3

Technological Change and Wage Inequality

The pronounced trend toward greater U.S. wage inequality after 1980 occurred at the same time as three other significant economic trends. These are the development and diffusion of digital information and communications technology, the rapid growth of world trade and capital movements between high-income economies and developing countries, particularly China, and the evolution of labor market institutions and policies in the U.S. that led to the reduced bargaining power of workers. While we must be careful not to assume that common trends imply causation, there are theoretical and empirical reasons to believe that the interaction of these important structural changes in the U.S. economy contributed to the rise in wage inequality documented in Chapter 2.

For the most part, economists regard the implementation of new technology in the production of goods and services as a principal source of improvements in a society's material standard of living through faster economic growth. Any required labor market adjustments are seen as the short-term unavoidable costs of these benefits. Here, we examine the potential impact of technological change on wage inequality as one of these required labor market adjustments. The impact of the trends to greater economic globalization and reduced bargaining power of workers will be considered in the following two chapters.

We can define technological change as the application of new knowledge gained by human ingenuity to the development of new products or new methods of producing existing products. Technology itself is very

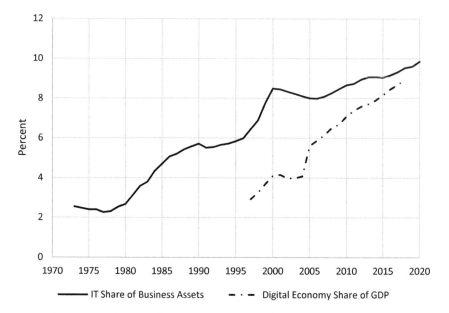

Figure 3.1:   Indicators of the Importance of IT in the U.S. Economy

Source: The IT share of business assets is calculated from data at https://apps.bea.gov/iTable/ReqID=1-&step=2. The Digital Economy Share of GDP is from data at https://www.bea.gov/data/special-topics/digital-economy.

difficult to measure, but Figure 3.1 provides two tangible indicators of the economic impact of digital technological change in the U.S. The first is an indicator of business use of digital technology in production. This tracks the share of total private business capital assets accounted for by computers, peripheral equipment and software, calculated from estimates of private fixed assets by the U.S. Department of Commerce, Bureau of Economic Analysis (BEA). The IT role in production increased dramatically over the period of rising wage inequality. In 1980, computer hardware and software accounted for a little more than 2% of business equipment, increasing to just about 10% in 2020.

The second indicator plotted in Figure 3.1 is the value of digital goods and services produced by the economy as a percentage of the value of all goods and services or GDP. This is also calculated from estimates by the BEA with available data from 1997 to 2018. The relative importance of digital goods and services also increased dramatically, rising from about 3% of GDP in 1997 to 9% in 2018. These two indicators of the growth of digital technology are closely correlated with measured wage inequality. The correlation coefficient between the U.S. 90/10 wage ratio and the hardware and software share of private business assets is 0.96 over the 1973–2020 period. Over the shorter 1997–2018 period, the correlation coefficient between the 90/10 wage ratio and output from the digital economy as a share of GDP is 0.90.

Economic analysis suggests a positive relationship between new digital technology and wage inequality stemming from the competition of new goods and services in product markets and a shift of labor demand in favor of the most skilled workers and against those workers whose jobs involve routine tasks. The high correlation between wage inequality and the measures of IT adoption shown in Figure 3.1 certainly provides support for these hypotheses. Much of the discussion about technology focuses on IT because of the prominence of information and communications technology in our daily lives. However, other technologies, including advances in science, medicine and managerial techniques, have also increased rapidly over the period since 1980 and would be expected to have similar effects on the labor market.

3.1. Creative Destruction

Joseph Schumpeter (1942) used the term "creative destruction" to describe the process of competition in capitalistic product markets. Entrepreneurs, attracted by the prospect of better-than-average profits, have an incentive to create new products that have greater appeal to consumers. If successful, these new products compete away customers of existing sellers, destroying the demand for older products. Since the demand for labor is derived from the demand for the goods and services labor helps to produce, the competitive process thus creates jobs with innovative producers of new products and destroys jobs at existing firms. Spencer and Kirchhoff (2006) examine how the process of creative destruction has been at work in the emergence of new technology-based companies in the U.S. economy.

An example of the way technological change disrupts labor markets in this process of competitive creative destruction can be seen in the impact of the growth of the Internet and, especially, smartphones on the producers of printed information. It seems clear from anecdotal evidence that the diffusion of these new technologies has had an adverse effect on the producers of such products as newspapers, catalogs, road atlases and city directories. But a close look reveals that the impact on jobs and pay has been quite severe.

Consider the employment of production and nonsupervisory workers in the printing and related support activities industry of the U.S. economy. Some industry-specific job titles for these workers are writers and editors, proofreaders and copy markers, printing press operators, binding and finishing workers, and etchers and engravers. According to the BLS,[1] employment of these workers totaled 595,600 in January 1990 and 578,300 in January 2000. After the turn of the century, and the introduction of the iPhone in 2007 and other smartphones thereafter, the number employed fell sharply. In January 2020, before the COVID-19 pandemic roiled the U.S. economy, production and nonsupervisory workers in this industry held just 282,500 jobs. This loss of nearly 300,000 printing-related jobs over a 20-year period illustrates part of the "destruction" associated with the creation of competitive new products through applications of new digital technology.

As we might expect from such a large decrease in employment, the wages earned by production and nonsupervisory workers in the printing and related support activities sector also suffered. Measured in terms of January 2020 consumer prices, the average hourly earnings of these workers fell from $21.25 at the beginning of 2000 to $19.44 in January 2020. The real average hourly earnings of these workers were 5% higher than the average hourly earnings of all U.S. production and nonsupervisory workers at the beginning of 2000 and fully 18% below this benchmark in January 2020.

The technological advances of the last 40 years have led to the development of many highly desirable new consumer or business products. It's difficult to imagine how we coped before the diffusion of the Internet and without a smartphone in our pockets. The clear advantages to consumers, however, come at a cost beyond the amount of money we have to pay for hardware, software and network access. As illustrated by our example above, one cost is the destruction of jobs and downward pressure on wages in other sectors of the economy that could contribute to an increase in wage inequality among workers. The open question is the manner in which the workers displaced by the job destruction aspect of technology are re-employed.

---

[1] See https://beta.bls.gov/dataViewer/view/timeseries/CEU3232300001.

3.2. Skill-Biased Technological Change

Rather than the role of new technology in creating a competitive advantage in new products, economic analysis of the link between technological change and wage inequality has focused mainly on technology as a factor of production. Economists view the production of goods and services as the result of the interaction of labor, capital and technology in the form of a production function. Think of the production of chocolate chip cookies in which labor, in the form of the baker, uses capital, in the form of the kitchen, oven and various utensils, and technology, in the form of the recipe and, perhaps, embodied in the latest kitchen gadgets, to transform raw materials into a finished, consumable product.

There are two key characteristics of this production function idea. One is that increased capital (more tools) and new technology (better recipes) can increase the productivity of labor by allowing a worker to produce more output in a given period of time. The second is that the combination of labor, capital and technology is not fixed but can change in proportions. Perhaps not in your kitchen but certainly in a commercial bakery, capital and technology can be substitutes for labor. We would be surprised to see cookies being made by 20 bakers in 20 conventional kitchen ovens in a large commercial bakery. Rather a couple of workers operating a continuously moving conveyor through a large oven that can be quickly adjusted for different products would be more likely. These two characteristics – more capital and better technology augmenting labor productivity but also substituting for labor in some cases – underlie the hypothesis of skill-biased technological change (SBTC).

With two types of labor, skilled and unskilled, the SBTC hypothesis argues that technological change will affect each type of labor differently. New technology is seen as greatly enhancing the productivity of skilled workers which leads to an increased demand for their services. In the case of unskilled workers, new technology increases the possibilities of substituting other inputs, perhaps through automation via technology-enhanced new capital equipment, in a way that offsets to some extent their increased productivity and limits increases in the demand for the unskilled. So, technological change is hypothesized to increase the demand for skilled workers relative to the demand for unskilled workers. Unless the supply of skilled labor increases along with the demand for skilled labor, SBTC would widen the gap between skilled and unskilled wages, thereby leading to an increase in wage inequality.

Evidence for the SBTC hypothesis is seen in the movement of the wage differential between college graduates and those with just a high-school diploma. This wage differential increased during the period of rising wage inequality since 1980. For example, information from the Economic Policy Institute (EPI) State of Working America Data Library shows that the bachelor's degree versus high school hourly wage advantage for workers over 16 years of age grew from 25.9% in 1980 to 47% in 2000 and 49.4% in 2019. These estimates control for gender, race, ethnicity, age and geographic area in addition to education. Research studies by Autor, Goldin and Katz (2020) and Hoffmann, Lee and Lemieux (2020) both estimate that the rise in the college wage premium could have accounted for slightly more than half of the overall increase in U.S. wage inequality from 1980 to 2019. As you might expect, these wage comparisons widen considerably if we compare those with advanced degrees to high school dropouts.

Recall that the SBTC impact on wage inequality depends not only on the degree to which technology spurs the demand for skilled labor but also on the degree to which the supply of skilled workers changes over the same time period. Even if technological change leads to a sharp rise in demand for those with certain skills, the effect of this on wages might well be muted, as it was in the 1970s, by an equally strong increase in the number of workers possessing those skills. In fact, Goldin and Katz (2008) trace the post-1980s rise in the college wage premium as much to slower growth in the supply of college-educated workers as to an acceleration in the technology-fueled growth in the demand for skilled workers. They estimate that the relative supply, as measured by the ratio of college to noncollege workers, increased at a rate of 3.8% from 1960 to 1980 but slowed markedly to 2.0% from 1980 to 2005, while the demand for college-educated workers relative to those without a college degree increased at about the same pace in both time periods.

A similar conclusion is reached by Autor, Goldin and Katz (2020) who attribute two-thirds of the rise in the college wage premium from 1979 to 2017 to a slowdown in relative supply growth and one-third to the increase in the pace of relative demand growth. An interesting perspective is provided by Hershbein, Kearney and Pardue (2020) who develop a statistical model of the U.S. labor market and use it to simulate the effect of the supply of college-educated workers on wage inequality from 1979 to 2018. In this exercise, they examine the impact if the rate of growth in bachelor's degree recipients had been 60% over those years instead of the actual rate of 45%. The model predicts that this faster rate of increase in the relative supply of skilled workers would have lowered slightly the 2018 90/50 wage ratio for men from 2.44 to 2.3 and for women from 2.22 to 2.20.

Why did the growth in the supply of college-educated workers slow down after 1980 when the college wage premium was rising, at times at a double-digit rate? One possibility is that, with roughly 70% of high school graduates starting college in recent years and 40% of those who matriculate receiving degrees, the U.S. is approaching a natural ceiling for the fraction of the population able and willing to achieve a bachelor's degree (Milanovic 2016). Additionally, attention has been drawn to the impact of steady tuition increases on the decision to enroll in college.

Tuition at private (public) higher educational institutions was 20% (4%) of median family income in the pre-1980 era but rose to 45% (10%) by 2005 (Goldin and Katz 2008). A recent paper by Levine, Ma and Russell (2020) shows that a 10% increase in tuition would lead to a 1.8% drop in the likelihood that individuals might apply for admission to a specific school, even though few students actually pay the "sticker price" tuition because of financial aid. In the public sector, tuition hikes have been one response to reduced state budget appropriations for higher education (Bound *et al.* 2019). Other responses, especially among less selective state universities, have included increased student–faculty ratios and reduced educational expenditures per student which have adversely affected college completion rates (Bound, Lovenhem and Turner 2010; Mitchell, Leachman and Saenz 2019).

One source of growing wage inequality, then, has been the growth in the wage premium for someone with a college degree relative to a worker with a high school diploma, which slowed considerably after 2000. It is also important to note that wage inequality *among* bachelor's degree recipients has also increased. BLS data for full-time workers over the age of 25 show that the 90/10 wage ratio for those with a bachelor's degree increased by 13.3% from 4.05 in 2000 to 4.59 in 2019 while the 90/10 wage ratio for workers with an advanced degree increased by 18.9% from 3.81 in 2000 to 4.53 in 2019. The 90/10 wage ratio for those with a high school diploma and no college rose at a much slower pace of 6.1% from 2000 to 2019.

Rising within-group inequality can be fitted into the SBTC framework if technological change increased the demand for the most skilled workers, perhaps measured by major, type of school or personal characteristics, among those with a bachelor's or advanced degree. Hoxby (2009) documents a trend toward increased polarization among colleges with the most able students, as measured by SAT scores, increasingly concentrated at the most selective institutions and all institutions becoming more homogeneous with respect to student characteristics. While seats at highly selective colleges increased slightly from 1962 to 2007, most of the increase in college enrollments over that time span was at less selective schools, where standards for admission have been falling.

With peer factors as an important aspect of education, the increased concentration of students with greater potential would enhance learning in more selective schools and contribute to greater differentiation in the labor market between students with similar degrees from more and less selective institutions. In addition, growing wage inequality among college graduates might well have contributed to the slowdown in the supply of college-educated workers as those unable to gain admission to the most selective schools faced less attractive wage returns to their ever more costly educational investment.

Finally, while CEO compensation is often traced to stock market performance and the deliberations of compensation committees of corporate boards, the SBTC hypothesis provides a possible productivity explanation for the remarkable rise in CEO compensation over the last 50 years. Improvements in information and communications technology may well have increased greatly the productivity of CEOs and other highly ranked corporate executives by increasing their span of control or the range of activities directly under their supervision. With nearly instantaneous access to relevant data and information and the ability to rapidly communicate decisions and monitor compliance, these officials can directly participate in the analysis and resolution of a larger array of corporate issues of strategic importance (Brynjolfson and McAfee 2016).

In such a situation, new technology will have increased the productivity of highly placed executives, as measured by the number and range of strategic decisions they make, thereby increasing their value to the firm. Competition among firms for the limited supply of individuals with the talent to fill these positions would raise their earnings just like competition for the limited supply of individuals with athletic talent has raised the earnings of professional athletes. In this vein, Tyson and Spence (2017) show that the extent to which firms adopt information technology is highly correlated with differences in executive earnings across firms and industries.

3.3. Job Polarization

SBTC provides an explanation for the sharp increases in top wages relative to the median that we observed in Chapter 2. However, it is less successful in explaining developments in the 50/10 wage differential, which involved faster wage growth for workers at the 10th percentile than for workers at the median for much of the period after 2010. As a result, researchers have increasingly turned to a task-based view of the production process to provide a theoretical description of the potential impact of technological change on the employment of capital and labor inputs (Autor 2013; Acemoglu and Restrepo 2018a).

In the task-based model, workers are seen as using capital equipment and technology to engage in specific tasks. Some tasks, such as the installation of windshields on an automobile assembly line, are directly connected to the production of goods and services. Other tasks, like planning and delivering worker training seminars, are indirectly connected to production. Specific jobs might involve workers in a single task while other jobs require the worker to engage in several different tasks. The efficient completion of all tasks, both direct and indirect, contributes to the profitability of the firm.

Tasks can be characterized along two dimensions (Jaimovich and Siu 2020). First, a task can be routine or nonroutine. A routine task is one that can be codified in that each step in the process of completing the task can be written down. The GPS system in your car or on your smartphone shows you how to complete the task of getting from point A to point B by following the directional steps given to you as you drive. Or a computer can be programmed to control the settings of a metal lathe or a 3D printer to produce a part for the assembly of a finished good. A nonroutine task is one in which it would be very difficult to prescribe a step-by-step process for its completion. Writing this paragraph is a nonroutine task. We have come to think of nonroutine tasks as difficult to complete via a computer program. However, artificial intelligence (AI)-powered computers can learn how to do nonroutine tasks. The much-discussed ChatGPT program could very well write this paragraph.

Tasks can also be differentiated by whether they require mainly cognitive or manual skills for their completion. Cognitive skills are those related to analysis and decision-making with uncertainty but also include the ability to effectively communicate, negotiate and persuade. Manual skills include strength, dexterity and adaptability. The preparation of a financial report for a meeting of the board of directors involves cognitive skills while making copies of the report and distributing them before the meeting largely requires manual skills. The task of repairing an automobile may require considerable cognitive ability as well as manual skills. In some self-managed work teams, there are situations in which any given team member might regularly perform both cognitive and manual tasks.

Because neither jobs nor tasks are identified in most data sets, researchers have attempted to categorize occupations into this four-fold classification using information provided by the U.S. Department of Labor's O*Net database and similar sources of information about the skill requirements of occupations maintained by other countries. For example, Foote and Ryan (2014) provide the following classification of a number of occupational groups routinely identified in the Current Population Survey and other widely used data sets:

- **Nonroutine cognitive (high skill)** – management, business and financial operations, and professional and related occupations.
- **Routine cognitive (middle skill)** – office and administrative support and sales occupations.
- **Routine manual (middle skill)** – production, transportation and material movement, construction and extraction, and installation, maintenance and repair occupations.
- **Nonroutine manual (low skill)** – service occupations.

Similar occupational classifications have been identified by other researchers. See, for example, the groupings used by Abel and Dietz (2020) and Atalay *et al.* (2020). A different approach is taken by Gaggl and Kaufmann (2020) who used statistical methods to identify clusters of tasks associated with detailed occupations that come very close to matching the judgmental identification of routine versus nonroutine occupational groups.

Technological change has two effects in this analysis of the production process. On the one hand, new technology creates new tasks and thereby increases the demand for labor. Acemoglu and Restrepo (2018a) point out that 60% of the total number of jobs created between 1980 and 2015 stemmed from occupations with new titles. An important historical example of this task-creation effect can be seen in the implementation of mass production techniques to take advantage of economies of scale in U.S. manufacturing firms in the period 1900–1930. Large-scale production created a need for information on production, sales, purchasing, finance, etc. so that managers could effectively manage large organizations. This in turn created a demand for clerks of all types and lower-level managers of these clerks to compile and report on this information. There was also a need for enhanced worker training and reduced turnover among workers who received costly training. As a result, firms expanded and professionalized human resource management and turned to internal labor markets with higher wages and benefits to provide an incentive for workers to stay with the firm (Kaufman 2001). The new tasks created by new mass manufacturing technology in the early 1900s played an important role in the decline in wage inequality during that period.

In addition to creating new jobs, new technology can also permit the automation of routine tasks that displaces workers from employment. While much of the recent research focuses naturally on the role of digital technology in automating jobs, there has always been a managerial interest in taking advantage of the "codifiability" of routine tasks to boost worker productivity and reduce the variability in quality that often comes with human labor. One example is the application of scientific management principles through time and motion studies to codify and control the behavior of workers on the job. The Jacquard loom, invented in 1804, with its chain of punch cards controlling the weaving process is an early precursor of digitally controlled machines automating routine tasks. In the current setting, the adoption of new information technology, fueled by a steady decline in the cost of computing, has changed the production process by creating new complex tasks that increase the demand for skilled labor and by automating routine tasks that reduce the demand for less skilled workers (Acemoglu and Restrepo 2018b).

It is argued that the net effect of the diffusion of information and communication technology over the last 40 years has been a hollowing out or polarization of the occupational structure in the U.S. and other high-income countries that has increased wage inequality (Autor 2015). In essence, new technology is seen as boosting the employment of those in high-skill, high-wage nonroutine cognitive jobs and lowering employment for those in middle-skill, middle-wage routine cognitive and manual jobs. In a way, this is very similar to the SBTC model discussed above. What differs is that this approach provides an explanation for the decline in wage inequality at the bottom of the wage distribution. The rapidly rising wages of high earners have increased the demand for services, from restaurant meals to landscaping and home maintenance to private security guards. This, in turn, has increased the demand for workers in the low-skill, low-wage nonroutine manual occupations where tasks are difficult to automate.[2] The shift of the job structure away from middle-level wage jobs toward both high- and low-wage jobs is a source of increased wage inequality among job holders.

Table 3.1 illustrates the way job polarization has affected the U.S. economy over the past two decades. The table uses data from the Occupational Employment and Wage Statistics program of the BLS[3] for major occupational groups. I followed Foote and Ryan (2014) in grouping occupations into the four task-related categories, providing more detailed data for the professional and related occupations they include in the non-routine cognitive group and for their service occupations in the nonroutine manual cluster. It is not clear whether the farming, fishing and forestry occupations belong to any of the four task-related categories. Data for that occupation are included in the total for all occupations but not separately reported. Average hourly earnings in 2019 for the nine nonroutine cognitive occupations was $41.04 while this figure was $20.48 for the six routine cognitive and manual occupations and $15.67 for the six nonroutine manual occupations.

The first data column in Table 3.1 details net job growth for each occupation and group for nearly two decades from 2001 to 2019. Almost all of the net employment growth occurred in the two nonroutine groups with nearly 11 million new nonroutine cognitive jobs and 9 million non-routine manual jobs created. In contrast, very little job growth occurred in the two routine categories. In fact, over 3 million office and administrative support jobs and 2 million production jobs were lost during that period. The only exception to this is the transportation and material movement occupation which added over 3 million new jobs from 2001 to 2019. The robust job growth in this occupation obviously reflects the growth of e-commerce during the same time frame. We can take a short drive from where I am writing this to several industrial parks where a large number of huge warehouses and fulfillment centers occupy space on what was farmland 20 years ago. With this one exception, it seems clear that the occupational structure of the U.S. workforce increasingly reflects

---

[2] As we will see in Chapter 5, the proliferation of state minimum wage laws also played an important role in wage determination at the 10th percentile.

[3] https://www.bls.gov/oes/tables.htm.

Table 3.1: Occupational Job Polarization 2001–2019

Occupation	Job Growth (in thousands) 2001–2019	Employment Share (%) 2001	2019	Annual Wage Share (%) 2001	2019	90/10 Wage Ratio 2001	2019
Nonroutine Cognitive							
Management	841.8	5.6	5.5	11.7	12.6	4.56	
Legal	241.4	0.7	0.8	1.4	1.6		
Architecture, Engineering	103.6	1.9	1.8	3.2	2.9	2.98	3.15
Business, Finance	3,507.1	3.6	5.6	5.4	8.1	3.14	3.23
Computer, Mathematics	1,727.0	2.2	3.1	3.9	5.4	3.05	3.35
Life, Physical Science	221.2	0.8	0.9	1.2	1.3	3.53	3.50
Healthcare Practitioners	2,554.2	4.8	5.9	7.0	9.2	3.82	4.17
Education	1,228.1	5.9	6.0	6.9	6.5	4.16	4.21
Arts, Design, Sports, Media, Entertainment	509.0	1.2	1.4	1.4	1.6	4.73	4.56
	10,933.4	**26.9**	**30.9**	**42.2**	**49.3**		
Routine Cognitive							
Sales	953.2	10.5	9.8	8.9	7.9	4.42	4.14
Office, Admin Support	−3,270.3	17.8	13.3	14.2	10.2	2.72	2.66
	−2,317.2	**28.3**	**23.1**	**23.2**	**18.1**		
Routine Manual							
Construction, Extraction	−45.3	4.9	4.2	5.1	4.1	3.15	3.02
Installation, Repair	390.4	4.2	3.9	4.3	3.6	2.99	2.97
Production	−2,111.2	8.8	6.2	7.1	4.7	3.01	2.73
Transportation	3,121.4	7.4	8.5	5.7	6.0	3.20	2.86
	1,355.2	**25.2**	**22.9**	**22.2**	**18.5**		
Nonroutine Manual							
Community Service	720.4	1.2	1.5	1.2	1.4	2.97	2.90
Protective Service	540.8	2.3	2.4	2.2	2.2	3.81	3.91
Health Care Support	3,398.9	2.4	4.4	2.2	2.6	2.24	2.17
Personal Care, Service	501.1	2.2	2.2	1.4	1.3	2.82	2.74
Cleaning, Maintenance	153.8	3.3	3.0	2.0	1.8	2.46	2.40
Food Prep and Serving	3,576.9	7.7	9.2	3.8	4.6	2.03	2.15
	8,892.0	**19.2**	**22.8**	**12.1**	**13.9**		
All Occupations	**18,895.1**	**100**	**100**	**100**	**100**	**4.47**	**4.69**

Note: Numbers for occupations may not add to totals (in bold) due to rounding. Blank cells indicate no available data.

Source: The Occupational Employment and Wage Statistics program of the Bureau of Labor Statistics at https://www.bls.gov/oes/tables.htm. See text for details.

polarization into high-wage and low-wage jobs and a hollowing out of occupations requiring middle-level skills and paying middle-level wages.

This conclusion is reinforced by the data on the total employment shares accounted for by each occupation. The share of jobs in the nonroutine cognitive cluster increased by 4 percentage points from 26.9% to 30.9% with business and financial operations occupations increasing their share of jobs by 2 full percentage points and the share held by health care providers and technicians rising by 1.1 percentage points. The share of total jobs also increased for occupations in the nonroutine manual task-related grouping, rising 3.6 percentage points from 19.2% to 22.8% with the biggest increase among healthcare support workers. Since the share of total employment must add to 100%, these increases were offset by a drop in the share of jobs in routine occupations from 53.5% to 46%.

The fourth and fifth columns of Table 3.1 document one of the effects of this change in the occupational job structure on wage inequality. Here, we calculate the share of total annual wages paid to workers in each occupation in 2001 and 2019. Wage inequality across these occupations in 2001 can be seen in the fact that the share of total wages going to those in high-paying nonroutine cognitive jobs was substantially higher than the share of all workers in these jobs. The reverse was true for all of the other occupations.

An increase in wage inequality between 2001 and 2019 can be seen in the fact that the share of wages paid to nonroutine cognitive workers increased between those years by 7.1 percentage points which was bigger than the increased share of jobs in these occupations. The rise in the share of annual wages going to high-paying jobs was matched by a decrease in the share of annual wages paid to those in routine jobs. This kind of shift would lead to a rise in the 90/50 wage ratio. The share of wages garnered by low-wage workers in nonroutine manual jobs also increased, albeit not as much as the share of employment. This shift would help explain the decrease in the 50/10 wage ratio noted in Chapter 2.

Thus, the shift of jobs and wages from middle-wage occupations to both high-wage and low-wage occupations would result in an increase in measured wage inequality. But there is another inequality-increasing factor exhibited in the changes documented in Table 3.1. The last two columns of the table show the extent of wage inequality *within* each occupation measured by 90/10 annual wage ratios for 2001 and 2019. While data are not available for the 90th percentile wage for managers in 2019 and for legal occupations in both years, it is sufficient to show that the shift of employment to nonroutine cognitive occupations was also a shift to occupations with generally higher within-group wage inequality that increased over time. For that category, the 90/10 ratio ranged from 2.98 to 4.73 in 2001 and increased from 2001 to 2019 in five of the seven occupations. Among the routine jobs, the 90/10 ratio ranged from 2.72 to 4.42 in 2001 and *decreased* for all occupations from 2001 to 2019. And among nonroutine manual occupations, the 90/10 ratio ranged from 2.03 to 3.81 in 2001 and rose in just two occupations from 2001 to 2019.

The data in Table 3.1, then, support two conclusions about the effect of occupational shifts in the U.S. economy over the past two decades. First, the shift of jobs and wage income away from middle-skill jobs to higher- and lower-skill jobs increased the inequality of wages across occupations. Second, the shift to higher paying nonroutine cognitive jobs was a shift toward occupations with generally greater within-occupation wage inequality that was rising over time. These occupational shifts and wage inequality results are consistent with the notion that rapid improvements in digital information and communications technology have been biased against routine jobs that can be eliminated through automation and in favor of high-skill workers who are complementary inputs with new technology and capital in production.

3.4. Summary

There is no doubt that the development and diffusion of digital information and communication technology over the past four decades have had a profound effect on the products and services we consume and on the manner in which they are produced. However, it is also the case that the adoption of new technology may have contributed to the rise in U.S. wage inequality over the same time period. An important question is what happened to the workers who were displaced by creative destruction or by the automation of routine occupations. If they were able to move fairly quickly into new jobs being created in response to new technology, then labor market disruptions might be considered a small price to pay for the benefits of new technology. Cortes (2016) gives us some optimistic evidence suggesting that moving from routine work to nonroutine cognitive jobs was more likely than moving from routine to lower-wage nonroutine maintenance jobs in the period 1990–2007. However, his data don't distinguish between those leaving routine jobs voluntarily and those displaced from routine jobs by automation or creative destruction. In the case of technology-driven job displacement, quick re-employment at comparable wages is unlikely to be the case since many of the new jobs require skills that are not held by many job losers. We will take this up in greater detail in considering the consequences of inequality but for now research clearly shows that, in general, displaced workers face long periods of unemployed job search with many ultimately opting to leave the labor force and those successfully finding new jobs doing so at substantially lower rates of pay.

Technological change has had a large effect on the U.S. labor market since 1980. It has helped fuel a steady increase in the demand for high-skilled labor that has been reflected in the wage premium received by college-educated workers and by the increased wage inequality among college-educated workers. Technological change has also facilitated the automation of routine jobs that contributed to the polarization of the workforce and a decline in the share of wages going to middle-skill workers. Both of these developments help explain the rise in the wage at the 90th percentile of the distribution and above. In addition, polarization is an important factor to consider in understanding the relative stagnation over time of the median wage. Those trying to forecast the future of work in America have speculated about the potential for AI to permit the automation of nonroutine cognitive jobs (Autor 2019). However, in the near term, it is likely that IT will continue to provide a mechanism for job polarization.

Chapter 4

Globalization

The prominent international economist Branko Milanovic has character-ized the decade just before the onset of the U.S. financial crisis and great recession in 2008 as "the most globalized years in human history" (Milanovic 2016, p. 18). He cites the levels and growth of international trade and financial transactions relative to world GDP in comparison with those prevailing during the past peak in globalization prior to World War I. He also notes the importance of the expansion of trade with China, India and the transition economies of central and eastern Europe. In addition to expanded trade in goods and services and increased international financial integration, we might usefully point to immigration flows and the emer-gence of global supply chains as additional indicators of the globalized economy.

Almost all economists would agree that a more integrated world economy would enhance economic efficiency by sourcing production from locations with a comparative advantage, directing capital to areas promising greater returns to investment and allocating labor to more pro-ductive uses. In fact, one prominent purpose of economic analysis since Adam Smith has been to demonstrate that the erection of barriers to global economic integration invariably leads to a lower standard of living for society. However, it is also a fact that economists feel the need to make that demonstration over and over, suggesting that the general public and political leaders need convincing about the gains from a more integrated world economy to weigh against the evident costs of globalization.

In this chapter, we consider the ways in which the various facets of globalization – trade, global supply chains, capital movements and immigration – may have contributed to rising wage inequality in U.S. labor markets. Fundamental economic analyses of the gains from a more open economy have always recognized that there are costs borne by some members of society who face particularly intense competition from imports, immigration and the relocation of production activities. However, these have generally been treated as short-term costs that are expected to be ameliorated by the reallocation of labor in a market economy. As we will see, recent research calls into question the short-term nature of globalization costs for affected individuals and their communities. Economic analyses have also recognized the potential for substantial gains to some producers and their employees from taking advantage of new export opportunities. These differential impacts of increased globalization have the effect of raising the wages of workers who gain and lowering the wages and employment opportunities of those who lose. The relative permanence of these adjustments is of particular interest to our study of wage inequality.

A consideration of globalization and its benefits and costs raises the very interesting question of how inequality among individuals around the world, high- and low-wage workers living in both high- and low-wage countries, has been affected. We close this chapter with an examination of the available evidence on who may have gained the most from the most globalized years in human history.

4.1. International Trade

A key indicator of globalization for the U.S. has been a significant increase in the importance of international trade in goods and services in general and trade with developing countries in particular. Key milestones along the way were the shift from fixed to flexible exchange rates in the mid-1970s, several rounds of free trade negotiations under the auspices of the World Trade Organization (WTO), the implementation of the North American Free Trade Agreement (NAFTA) in 1994 and China's entry into the WTO in 2001. Figure 4.1 illustrates the evolution of trade between the U.S. and the rest of the world (ROW) since 1950. Data are from the U.S. Bureau of Economic Analysis (BEA) with imports and exports expressed as a percentage of GDP.

We can identify four phases in the history of U.S. trade depicted in Figure 4.1. First, during the 1950s and 1960s, which by now we recognize

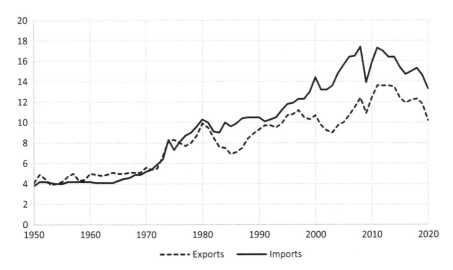

Figure 4.1: Exports and Imports as a Percentage of U.S. GDP, 1950–2020

Source: Bureau of Economic Analysis "Table 1.1.10 Percentage Shares of Gross Domestic Product" at https://apps.bea.gov/iTable/iTable.cfm?reqid=19&step=2#reqid=19&step=2&isuri=1&1921= survey.

as decades of low and stable wage inequality, exports and imports were nearly in balance and represented a fairly low fraction of U.S. economic output. In the second phase, the share of exports and imports in GDP began to rise fairly rapidly during the 1970s, with both reaching 10% by the end of the decade. In part, this reflected the oil price shocks during that period and the end of the fixed exchange rate international monetary system. Starting around 1975, the import share moved ahead of exports as a fraction of GDP, creating a balance of trade deficit that has continued until today.

The third phase encompasses the period of rapid globalization cited by Milanovic. After 1980, the import share of GDP grew rapidly, rising fairly steadily from about 10% of GDP in 1980 to nearly 18% of GDP in 2008 at the beginning of the financial crisis and great recession. Much of that acceleration in import growth occurred during the years from 1990 to 2008. The export share of GDP grew more slowly after 1980 and its progress was marked by deep decreases in the first half of the 1980s, when the trade-weighted exchange value of the dollar rose to a 1985 peak (Humpage and Karamouzis 1985), and during the downturn associated with the "dot com" bust in 2001. After the turn of the 21st century, exports as a share of GDP followed a very similar path to that of imports, albeit falling well below the import share every year. The U.S. balance of trade (exports minus imports) was in perennial deficit after 1975 with the magnitude of this deficit expanding sharply after 2000.

The fourth phase evident in Figure 4.1 is a retreat from the high rates of exports and imports that began during the great recession and continued, after a brief recovery in 2011, until the end of the decade in 2020. While predicting a resumption of globalization trends, James (2021) points to rising protectionist sentiment and increased political focus on promoting domestic economic recovery from the financial and pandemic crises as the reason for the pause in the pace of globalization after 2010. We can also point to the effects of the tariff increases from the "trade war" initiated by the Trump administration against China and other countries and the massive disruption of global shipping that began during the COVID-19 pandemic and continued into 2021. Both exports and imports as a fraction of GDP fell during the ten years from 2011 to 2020 but the balance of trade deficit remained largely unchanged over those years. This discussion makes clear that the rise in U.S. wage inequality occurred during a period of major changes in the economic relations between the U.S. and the ROW.

In addition to the data presented in Figure 4.1, the BEA also provides information on U.S. trade in goods with major trading partners for the years from 1999 to 2020.[1] These data point to the growing importance of imported goods from China and other developing countries in the years following the turn of the 21st century. While we have become accustomed to thinking of the U.S. trade deficit with China as a major part of our trade "problem", it is important to recognize that China accounted for just 7.9% of goods imported to the U.S. as recently as 1999. In the years following the turn of the century, this figure grew sharply, more than doubling to 18.5% of all U.S. imports in 2020. Looking beyond just China, imported goods from eight developing economies – Brazil, China, Hong Kong, India, Mexico, Singapore, South Korea and Taiwan – were 29.8% of U.S. imports in 1999 and 43.2% in 2020. These eight countries also increased their purchases of goods exported from the U.S., albeit at a slower pace

---

[1] U.S. Bureau of Economic Analysis, Table 2.2. U.S. International Trade in Goods by Area and Country, Seasonally Adjusted. https://apps.bea.gov/iTable/iTable.cfm?ReqID=62&step=1#reqid=62&step=9&isuri=1&6210=4 (Accessed 10/28/21).

than U.S. imports of goods produced by them. The percentage of U.S. goods exported to these economies rose from 27% in 1999 to 37.1% in 2020. Putting these import and export trends together, we find that the deficit in the balance of trade in goods between the U.S. and these eight developing economies rose from –$120.4 billion in 1999 to –$484.7 billion in 2020 with the share of this deficit accounted for by China rising from 57.1% to 63.9%.

An increase in trade between developing countries and high-income countries like the U.S. has important implications for wage inequality. For example, the highly influential trade theory developed by Stolper and Samuelson (1941) hypothesizes that increased trade between a high-income country, with a relative abundance of skilled workers, and a low-income country, with a comparative advantage in unskilled labor, would raise inequality in the former and reduce it in the latter. Elhanan Helpman (2018) provides a comprehensive review of more recent theoretical models of the links between trade and labor markets. A general conclusion of this theoretical research is that increased trade, particularly with low-income countries, would widen the wage gap between skilled and unskilled workers in countries like the U.S. In addition, models based on efficient matching of firms with workers who differ by skills find that larger, more productive firms choose to compete in export markets. As a result, they gain in terms of market size, which enhances their profitability. The potential gains from expanding export markets lead them to expand employment and offer higher wages in order to attract the most skilled and productive workers. These matching models predict that wage gaps by skill would rise in both high- and low-income countries as a result of increased trade.

Professor Helpman (2018) also reviews the growing research literature that has attempted to test the hypotheses regarding trade and wage inequality derived from theoretical models. His reading of the empirical studies leads to the conclusion that in recent decades the expansion of international trade with low-income economies is indeed correlated with increased wage differentials by skill in the U.S. and other high-income countries. However, the magnitude of the trade impact on the wages of skilled workers relative to unskilled workers appears to be rather small. An example is seen in Lee (2020), whose empirical analysis focuses on the period from 2000 to 2007 when manufacturing exports from China increased rapidly. Concentrating on the results he reports for the U.S., the decrease in bilateral trade costs, from reduced policy barriers and lower transportation costs, is estimated to have increased the U.S. college-high school wage ratio by 0.5% while lower prices for Chinese manufactured goods due to increased productivity growth in that country may have added 0.3% to this skill differential. This is a pretty small estimate of the wage effects of what was a massive increase in U.S. trade with China.

It is important to recognize that the expansion of trade with low-wage economies has two reinforcing instead of offsetting effects on wage inequality: On the one hand, there is an increase in the export market for the high-quality products and services produced by U.S. firms employing largely high-skilled labor. For example, U.S. exports of financial services grew by 481% between 2000 and 2019.[2] As these firms export more, the demand for high-skilled labor rises and wages are bid up. On the other hand, import competition from producers in China and other countries with a relative abundance of low-skilled labor would depress the demand for low-skilled labor in the U.S. and similar countries. These changes in the skilled wage premium would be reinforced by differences in the opportunities for re-employment available to workers affected by import-related job losses. Job losers with a college education find it easy to move fairly quickly into higher-paying nonroutine cognitive jobs in the expanding export firms or in the service sector while those with less education reallocate to lower-paying jobs in nonroutine manual occupations (Lee 2020).

The fact that there are winners and losers from freer international trade is not surprising. The basic economic model of the effect of imports on domestic producers clearly shows that to be the case, at least in the short run. Over time, economic growth, in part resulting from the efficiencies gained as a result of trade-induced shifts of labor and other resources to more productive uses, is expected to diminish these short-run costs. The fact that researchers looking at the nation as a whole find a small estimated effect of increased trade on wage inequality is a comfortable outcome for economists who believe strongly that the gains from free trade outweigh the costs (Wood 2018). However, recent research on the local effects of rapid growth in U.S. imports from China and other low-wage economies calls into question the notion that the labor market effects of international trade are small and relatively short-lived.

Close consideration has been given to the research along these lines for the years from 1990 to 2007 by Autor, Dorn and Hanson (2013),

---

[2]U.S. Bureau of Economic Analysis, Table 2.1 U.S. Trade in Services, by Type of Service. https://apps.bea.gov/iTable/iTable.cfm?ReqID=62&step=1.

updated to 2019 in Autor, Dorn and Hanson (2021). They use the variation in Chinese imports across industries and differences in the industrial composition of manufacturing employment across local labor markets to study the effect of imports from China on local labor outcomes. Local labor markets are measured by commuting zones that cluster counties according to the extent to which commuting to work crosses county lines. Exposure to Chinese import competition is measured by changes in the dollar value of U.S. imports in each manufacturing industry multiplied by the share of that industry's employment located in a given commuting zone and divided by the total number of commuting zone workers in that industry at the beginning of the period.[3] These industry-specific totals are then summed across all manufacturing industries. For the years of rapid Chinese import growth from 2000 to 2007, the exposure of the median commuting zone to increased Chinese imports was $2,110 per worker. For the 90th percentile commuting zone, exposure was $4,300 per worker while the 10th percentile commuting zone had exposure equal to $1,030 per worker (Autor, Dorn and Hanson 2013).

How did this difference in exposure to Chinese imports affect labor market outcomes across the 722 commuting zones in the 48 contiguous states plus the District of Columbia? There are five major results from their research:

1. Greater exposure to increased Chinese imports accelerated the decline in the proportion of the working-age population employed in manufacturing jobs. Over the period from 1990 to 2019, import competition is estimated to account for over half of the average commuting zone's 2.8 percentage point decline in this proportion.
2. The accelerated loss of manufacturing jobs was not absorbed by faster growth of nonmanufacturing employment or by the outmigration of job losers. Instead, unemployment increased as did the percentage of the working-age population not in the labor force.

---

[3] A numerical example might help. Suppose U.S. imports of toys from China amounted to $1 million in a given year and that a particular commuting zone accounted for 1% of total U.S. employment in toy manufacturing and had total employment in toy production of 10,000. Exposure to Chinese imports in the toy industry in this commuting zone would be $1 per worker, calculated as ($1 million × .01)/10,000. The total exposure for this commuting zone would be the sum of the results from this type of calculation for all of the industries in the local economy.

3. Commuting zones with greater exposure to Chinese imports had slower growth in average weekly earnings that was, interestingly, concentrated in the nonmanufacturing sector.
4. The increased rates of nonemployment in areas facing greater import competition resulted in a significant increase in government transfer payments, largely social security and medical benefits to those residents. Trade adjustment assistance, designed to compensate workers for import-related job losses by providing federal funding for retraining and relocation, had a relatively small effect on family incomes in these commuting zones.
5. The negative consequences of sensitivity to Chinese imports were persistent, at least until 2019, even though the period of rapid growth in Chinese imports ended around 2010. The persistence of these consequences and their geographic concentration raise questions about the ability of local U.S. markets to adjust to the impact of increased trade of the size of the 2000–2010 burst of imports from China.

These papers don't directly examine the effect of increased exposure to imports from China on wage inequality, but we can infer what such an effect might look like from their results. For example, the evidence that import exposure was negatively related to average weekly earnings would result in a widening of wage differentials among localities that were differentially impacted by trade. And the increased loss of manufacturing jobs in areas with greater import exposure would have a big effect on the wages of low-skill workers. Because of higher productivity, most manufacturing jobs offer significantly higher wages to those with less than a college education. Indeed, Chetverikov, Larsen and Palmer (2016) find that increased trade with China had a larger negative effect on the wages of less-educated workers in cross-industry data. For these reasons, we would expect that the sharp rise in imports from China after 2000 would contribute to the increase in wage inequality observed after that date.

Figure 4.2 gives us a rough idea of how increased imports from China affected wage inequality. The chart presents a scatter plot of the change in import exposure from 2000 to 2007 and the change in the 90/10 wage ratio from 2001 to 2007 for the 48 contiguous states plus the District of Columbia. To get state-level estimates of exposure to Chinese imports, I simply added the data on imports per worker for the commuting zones

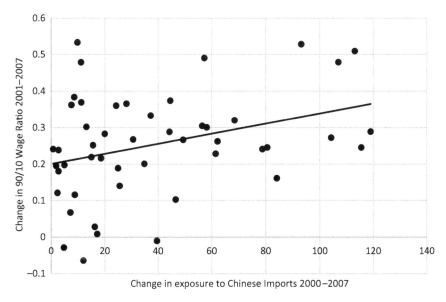

Figure 4.2:   Imports from China and Wage Inequality Across U.S. States

Sources: Import exposure is from Autor, Dorn and Hanson (2013) and is available at https://www. openicpsr.org/openicpsr/project/112670/version/V1/view. The change in the 90/10 wage ratio is from data at https://www.bls.gov/oes/tables.htm. See text for details.

centered in each state from Autor, Dorn and Hanson (2013).[4] This measure ranges from $119,000 per worker in Tennessee to $800 per worker in DC with an average of $38,000 per worker across the sample. The change in the 90/10 wage ratio data comes from the Occupational Employment and Wage Statistics program of the BLS at https://www.bls.gov/oes/tables.htm and is for workers in all occupations. From 2001 to 2007,[5] the 90/10 ratio increased by 0.50 or more points in Georgia, New Mexico and Texas and fell slightly in Arizona, New York and Vermont. Across all 48 states and the District of Columbia, the 90/10 ratio increased, on average, by 0.25 points from 2001 to 2007.

---

[4]I aggregate to the state level because wage inequality data are not readily available for commuting zones. Data used in their paper are available as a supplement to the article on the website of the *American Economic Review* and can be accessed at https://www. openicpsr.org/openicpsr/project/112670/version/V1/view.

[5]Wage inequality data for workers in all occupations start in 2001.

Figure 4.2 demonstrates a close positive relationship between exposure to Chinese imports and increases in wage inequality across the 50 states and DC. States with a greater exposure to increased imports from China in the years from 2000 to 2007 also had a bigger increase in wage inequality, as measured by the change in the 90/10 wage ratio, in the same period. A $10,000 bigger increase in Chinese imports per worker is predicted to add 0.014 to the change in the 90/10 wage ratio. If we start at the variable means, which by construction make up a point on the fitted line, this amounts to a 5.5% increase in the change in the 90/10 wage ratio in response to a 26% increase in import exposure. So, the effect is not all that big. In addition, the estimated linear relationship indicates that variation across the states in increased import exposure from China can explain only about 11% of the variation in the change in wage inequality. Clearly, other factors, in addition to increased import competition from China, had a role to play in the rise in wage inequality in each jurisdiction over the 2001–2007 period.

At one point, there was a keen debate among many economists over whether trade **or** technology was the primary determinant of rising wage inequality. Given our brief review of the theoretical literature and empirical results, it seems more correct to say that trade **and** technology are both determinants of rising wage inequality but the impact of trade may be modest and concentrated on import-sensitive communities.

4.2. Offshoring

Offshoring is another aspect of globalization that has implications for U.S. wage inequality. This involves decisions of U.S. business firms to locate some of the tasks involved in producing a product or service in another country. An example would be locating the production of a component in, say, China and importing that component to the U.S. for assembly into the finished product. The attraction of offshoring production tasks to low-income countries is the possibility of lowering average cost, by taking advantage of an ample supply of low-wage labor and limited foreign government regulation of labor conditions, and increasing overall profitability. However, a deterrent to offshoring is the fixed cost associated with shifting production tasks to another country. These might include costs of meeting legal and political requirements for operating there, costs of establishing a relationship with local firms or directly investing in production facilities and costs of monitoring production and transporting the product to the home country (Timmer *et al.* 2014). The same combination of policy changes and reductions in communications and transportation costs that fueled the rise in international trade after the turn of the 21st century also helped reduce this fixed cost deterrent to offshoring. As an example of the significance of transportation costs to the offshoring decision, we can point to the way that the increased cost of shipping a container during the COVID-19 pandemic has led many firms to reconsider the advantages of offshoring (Shih 2020).

It's important to note the difference between imports resulting from international trade and the imports associated with offshoring. In the former case, decisions to sell goods or services in the U.S., say, are made by foreign companies and imports present new competition to domestic firms. The negative effects of import competition on U.S. workers and their communities discussed above result from the comparative advantage of low-wage countries in the production of certain goods and services. In the case of offshoring, it is U.S. firms that decide to shift certain production tasks to foreign countries and import the products of that activity to the U.S. Rather than facing new competition, U.S. firms adopt offshoring as a strategy to lower costs and boost profits. The effect on business firms differs considerably even if low-wage U.S. workers are adversely affected in similar ways.

Figure 4.3 gives us a glimpse of the evolution of U.S. offshoring in manufacturing and other industries over the first two decades of the 21st century. The figure charts imports into the U.S. that were shipped by foreign affiliates to their U.S. parent companies divided by the total sales of the parent companies. This is constructed from data on the activities of multinational companies collected by the Bureau of Economic Analysis. Among manufacturing firms, imports from foreign affiliates rose steadily from a bit more than 5% of sales in 1999 to 7.4% in 2016, after which they fell slightly ending at 7.2% of sales in 2019. While the increase in imports from foreign affiliates might look modest as a percentage of sales, in dollar terms, they rose by 146% from 1999 to 2019. For nonmanufacturing U.S. multinational firms, imports shipped from foreign affiliates amounted to less than 1% of sales with no discernible trend over these two decades.

Information on employment trends in manufacturing reinforces this picture of an increasing importance of foreign affiliates to their U.S. parents. Total employment at parent firms of U.S. manufacturing multinational firms fell from around 9 million workers in 1999 to 7.5 million

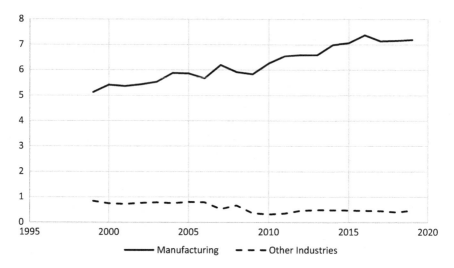

Figure 4.3: Imports from Foreign Affiliates as a Percentage of Sales for U.S. Multinational Firms

Source: U.S. Bureau of Economic Analysis data on activities of multinational firms available at https://apps.bea.gov/iTable/iTable.cfm?ReqID=2&step=1.

workers in 2019. This parallels the overall drop in manufacturing jobs in the U.S. economy after the turn of the century although the job decline was smaller at multinational firms. Total U.S. manufacturing employment growth was –26% from 1999 to 2019 while the rate of change for manufacturing multinationals over the same period was –17.5%. At the same time, total employment at the foreign affiliates of U.S. manufacturing multinational firms rose by 28%, from 5.3 million workers in 1999 to 6.8 million in 2019. Clearly, whether measured in terms of imports or employment, offshoring increased in significance in the U.S. manufacturing sector in the two decades after 1999.

In thinking about the effect of offshoring on wage inequality, it's worth noting the likely role the shifting of tasks overseas might have played in the process of job polarization discussed in the previous chapter. It seems logical that the easiest tasks to submit to a foreign affiliate and then monitor from afar would be routine tasks that can be readily described in step-by-step instructions. Cavenaile (2021) finds that U.S. job polarization increased from 1975 to 2008 both because of the decreasing costs of offshoring leading to the spread of global supply chains and the effect of IT innovations on automation. Interestingly, his results show that computerization and automation were relatively more important from 1975 to around 1990 while offshoring became the main driver of job polarization, and the resulting increase in wage inequality, after 1990.

The comprehensive review of the literature on the labor market impact of offshoring by Hummels, Munch and Xiang (2018) also finds that a common result seen in several studies is that wages and employment in routine occupations are particularly affected by offshoring. They also note that studies on data across industries over time, on data across firms over time and on data linking individual workers to their employers over time show consistent negative correlations between measures of offshoring and average wage levels and employment. With regard to worker skills, negative wage effects of offshoring are estimated for less-skilled workers while wage effects are often positive for those with greater skills, many of whom are engaged in managing global supply chains. Finally, they review a few studies showing that workers who were displaced from their jobs by offshoring decisions faced prolonged periods of increased unemployment and sharply lower real wages in the years after their job loss.

Finally, Matilde Cardoso and her colleagues (2021) conducted a meta-analysis of the estimated effects of offshoring on wages. Meta-analysis applies statistical techniques to statistical estimates in order to determine the reliability, in probability terms, of general conclusions about the sign and significance of the relationship between variables. They examined 759 estimates of the relationship between offshoring and wages reported in 30 published research papers and note that there is strong support for the conclusion that offshoring has a positive effect on the wages of high-skill workers and a negative effect on the wages of those with lesser skills. The positive effect on high-skill wages reflects the improvements in profitability made possible by offshoring tasks to low-wage countries and the enhanced employment of managers and technical personnel needed to fully implement a global supply chain. The qualitative review of the literature by Hummels *et al.* (2018) and the quantitative review of the literature via meta-analysis by Cardoso *et al.* (2021) both suggest an important role for offshoring as a determinant of increased U.S. wage inequality.

4.3. International Financial Flows

Along with international trade in goods and services and the extent of global supply chains, international financial flows expanded dramatically during the period of enhanced globalization from about 1980 to the financial crisis in 2008. Innovations in information and communications technology made it easier to identify and carry out promising financial investments in far-flung locations. In parallel with policies that liberalized trade, many governments around the globe removed restrictions on the free flow of investment funds across borders. In a report by the McKinsey Global Institute, Farrell *et al.* (2009) estimate that the value of total global financial assets (equities, government and private debt, and deposit accounts) rose from about $12 trillion, about equal to global GDP, in 1980 to $196 trillion, equal to 3.5 times global GDP, in 2007. This rapid increase reflects the dramatic increase in international financial flows during the decades when U.S. wage inequality was rising.

Balance of payments accounting links the financial flows between countries to trade in goods and services. For a country like the U.S. with a balance of trade deficit (imports of goods and services are greater than exports), this will be offset by a surplus on the capital account (purchases of U.S. real and financial assets by foreigners are greater than purchases of assets abroad by U.S. residents). This balance of payments condition will be maintained by movements in exchange rates. In the U.S. case, where the dollar is the global reserve currency and many global prices are set in terms of dollars, the decisions of banks, businesses and others abroad to hold dollars to facilitate their transactions will also help offset the trade deficit with a capital account surplus. A look back at Figure 4.1 reminds us that the U.S. has registered a negative trade balance every year since 1975, with the gap between imports and exports widening significantly in the period from 1997 to the onset of the financial crisis and great recession in 2008. In the recovery from the great recession up to the COVID-19 pandemic, the U.S. trade deficit narrowed a bit but still amounted to about 3% of GDP.

The balance of payments condition has often been described as the U.S. borrowing from the ROW in order to pay for importing more from the ROW than we sell to it. This views the capital account as a kind of national credit card account, running up balances each year to cover purchases in excess of our income. The strong implication of this characterization is that this situation is not sustainable and requires the U.S. to increase exports and or decrease imports. But this is too simplistic. The transactions involved in "ROW purchases of U.S. assets" include Subaru investing in its Indiana assembly plant, the Saudi Arabian Sovereign Wealth Fund taking a position in a New York hedge fund, Russian oligarchs and Chinese billionaires buying real estate in Manhattan or Miami, and European banks buying U.S. government bonds for the portfolios of their clients. It is difficult to link the decisions behind such transactions to the U.S. trade deficit.

An alternative view is that the U.S. has a global comparative advantage in the depth, breadth and liquidity of its financial markets and that the rise in the trade deficit during the period of rapid globalization was partially caused by ROW purchases of U.S. financial and real assets. An increase in the demand for U.S. assets by those who live and do business in other countries would bid up the exchange rate value of the dollar relative to other currencies. This would lower the cost of importing goods to the U.S. (since the dollar now can buy more pounds and euros) and increase the cost of U.S. goods to foreign buyers (since they now have to surrender more pounds and euros to obtain the dollars required for these purchases).

Support for this view of the relationship between trade deficits and net ROW purchases of U.S. assets is provided by Joseph Steinberg's (2019) sophisticated general equilibrium model and wedge accounting exercise calibrated to match data for the 1995–2011 period. He finds that a global savings glut (domestic savings in excess of profitable local investment opportunities) was the primary driver of the large increase in the U.S. trade deficit, explaining much of the observed cumulative increase during his sample period. Steinberg also points to this savings glut as the primary driver of the observed 25% increase in the real exchange value of the dollar from 2000 to 2011. This rise in the value of the dollar relative to other currencies, which would make U.S. exports more expensive and imports cheaper, helps explain the link between the inflow of global savings to U.S. capital markets and an increased trade deficit. Note that we are talking about an increase in the foreign exchange value of the dollar during a period in which the U.S. consistently ran a big trade deficit.

It is the inflow of global savings to U.S. capital markets and the resulting impact on the demand for highly skilled workers in the financial services sector that provide a third channel by which globalization may have affected U.S. wage inequality. Figure 4.4 illustrates the role of exports of financial services in the evolution of the U.S. financial sector over the years from 1999 to 2020, charting exports of finance and insurance services as a fraction of industry output and the value of finance and insurance services as a percentage of GDP.

The value of financial and insurance services produced and sold in the U.S. (for example, the revenue earned by U.S. firms from providing bank

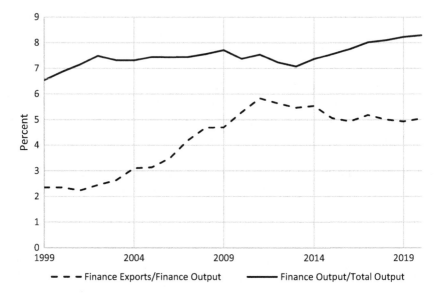

Figure 4.4:   Exports and Output of U.S. Finance and Insurance Services

Sources: U.S. Bureau of Economic Analysis Industry Economic Accounts at https://apps.bea.gov/ iTable/iTable.cfm?reqid=150&step=2&isuri=1&categories=gdpxind and Table 3.1 U.S. International Trade in Services at https://apps.bea.gov/iTable/iTable.cfm?ReqID=62&step=1#reqid=62&step=9&i suri=1&6210=4.

deposits and loans, managing stock and bond issuance, consulting on mergers and acquisitions, advising on retirement wealth management or providing sophisticated insurance products) increased at a fairly steady pace as a percentage of the value of all goods and services from 6.5% in 1999 to slightly more than 8% in 2019 and 2020. However, a very different picture emerges of the value of the same types of financial and insurance services produced and sold to foreign individuals or businesses by U.S. financial institutions. Initially, exports relative to the total output of financial services rose dramatically from just over 2% in 1999 to nearly 6% in 2011 after which they declined slightly ending at around 5% in 2019 and 2020. The initial period reflects the height of globalization and the expansion of U.S. trade with China with the resulting increase in both the trade deficit and financial flows into the U.S. As we have seen, after the great recession, the impetus to globalization waned and, as a result, international financial flows decreased.

The growth of financial services in general and the rapid growth of financial services exports during the period of expanding globalization are important for wage inequality because financial services workers, along with top-level managers in all industries, dominate the top 10% and top 1% of wage earners. For example, Bell and van Reenen (2013) find that, in the U.K., employees in the financial services sector accounted for 60% of the increase in the share of total wage and salary payments going to the top 1% of wage earners from 1998 to 2007. Similar results for the U.S. financial sector are seen in the detailed examination of private equity firms by Phallippou (2020).

An interesting study by Phillipon and Reshef (2012) examines wages and skills in the U.S. finance industry from 1909 to 2006. They find evidence for a U-shaped evolution of the average and top 10% wage in finance relative to all private, nonfarm workers that matches quite closely the long-run U-shape in overall wage inequality. Average wages in finance were 1.5 times the average wages in all industries from 1909 until 1933. This figure then fell reaching a low point of 1.1 times the average wages in all industries that persisted from 1950 to 1980. After 1980, the relative wage in finance increased steadily to around 1.7 times the average earnings in all industries in 2006. They estimate that the increase in the college wage premium in the U.S. finance sector alone can account for as much as one-quarter of the growth in the overall U.S. college wage premium after 1980.

Boustanifar, Grant and Reshef (2018) reach a similar conclusion. They calculate that the rising relative wage of educated workers in the finance sector accounted for 22% of the rise in the U.S. college wage premium from 1980 to 2005. While they find that financial deregulation was the primary driver of increased relative pay for financial services employees across 15 high-income countries, they also provide some evidence of a positive correlation between increases in financial globalization and relative earnings in finance. The increase in exports of financial services added to the effect of rising domestic demand for financial services in driving up the wages of highly-skilled, high-wage workers in the U.S. economy over the past 40 years.

4.4. Immigration

Perhaps the most politically contentious aspect of globalization is immigration. We need only consider the 2015 refugee crisis that faced the

European Union, the prominent role of immigration in the 2016 vote for Brexit, the intense focus of the 2016 Trump campaign and his administration on securing the U.S. border with Mexico against undocumented immigrants and restricting the entry of those from Central America claiming refugee status, and the 2020 refugee standoff at the border between Poland and Belarus to see the prominent role of immigration in current events.

The concerns are both economic and cultural. There is a strong belief that immigration adds significantly to the supply of labor, in particular the supply of low-skilled labor, and thereby reduces job opportunities and wage levels for native-born individuals. There is also deep concern that immigration will have adverse cultural effects and dilute the political power of native-born citizens. As a result, immigration remains tightly controlled by most governments and the rise of globalization has not had the same liberalizing influence on immigration policy as it has on trade policy and regulations on capital flows between countries. The key exception is the allowance for the free movement of people among the 26 European countries that are signatories to the Schengen Agreement.

In the U.S., the growth of the foreign-born population is correlated with the long-run evolution of wage inequality over time. Budiman (2020) shows that the percentage of the U.S. population born abroad peaked at nearly 15% in the period from 1890 to 1910, fell steadily from 1910 to a low of 4.7% in 1970 and then rose steadily to 13.7% in 2018. Once again, we find a U-shaped pattern that is clearly coincident with the U-shaped evolution of wage inequality over that same long time period.

Figure 4.5 plots the percentage of the U.S. labor force accounted for by foreign-born workers and job-seekers. The relative importance of immigrants in the U.S. supply of labor increased steadily after 1970. The pace of growth quickened a bit after 1980 and then slowed noticeably after the great recession, a period in which the number of unauthorized immigrants in the country is estimated to have fallen significantly. Even so, the immigrant percentage of the workforce more than tripled from 1970 to 2018 when, as we have seen, U.S. wage inequality also increased.

Budiman (2020) also provides detailed information about the characteristics of the foreign-born population residing in the U.S. Those in the country legally accounted for 77% of the foreign-born in 2018 and 35% were naturalized citizens. Immigrants authorized to reside in the U.S. accounted for more than a third of the 11.2 million people added to the U.S. labor force in the ten years from 2007 to 2017, while the number of

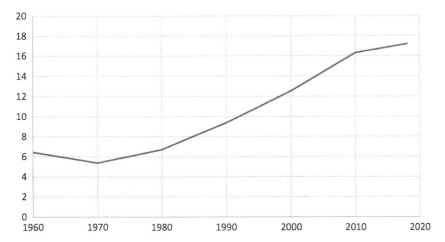

Figure 4.5: Foreign-Born Workers as a Percentage of the U.S. Labor Force

Source: Pew Research Center at https://www.pewresearch.org/hispanic/2020/08/20/facts-on-u-s-immigrants-trend-data/.

unauthorized foreign-born in the workforce is estimated to have fallen by 600,000 during that period. Measured by educational attainment, immigrants are both low-skill and high-skill workers. In 2018, 32% of the foreign-born and 33% of the native-born had at least a bachelor's degree, while 27% of the foreign-born and 8% of the native-born had less than a high school diploma. This complicates the analysis of the effects of immigration on wage inequality since the foreign-born are potentially adding to the labor supply in both high-wage and low-wage markets.

Given the policy concerns discussed above, a large literature has emerged on the labor market effects of immigration on native-born workers with a pronounced emphasis on the effects in low-skill markets. The National Academies of Sciences, Engineering, and Medicine commissioned a blue-ribbon panel to review this large literature plus that on the fiscal effects of immigration on government budgets. The report, edited by Francine Blau and Christopher Mackie (2017), provides a clear and comprehensive examination of the various attempts to identify the causal effect of immigration on American labor markets. The report reaches two main conclusions. First, an influx of immigrants into low-skill geographical or occupational labor markets has a negative effect on wages with the biggest impact on previous cohorts of immigrants and native-born high school dropouts. The negative wage effect is smaller for estimates over longer periods, say a decade rather than a year, as the market has more time to adjust to the inflow of new workers. The range of estimates is wide, with a 1% increase in labor supply due to immigration linked to native-born wage changes of 0% to −1.7%.

Second, the few studies of the labor market effect of highly educated immigrants often find small positive wage effects on native-born workers. This reflects the fact that most highly educated immigrants generally have degrees in STEM disciplines and may be complements rather than substitutes for native-born highly educated workers. These conclusions suggest that an influx of immigrants would increase wage inequality by reducing low-skill wages below the level they would otherwise reach and by increasing high-skill wages.

David Card shared the 2021 Nobel Prize in Economics partly because of his innovative empirical work on the labor market effects of immigration. In his Richard T. Ely lecture at the 2009 meeting of the American Economic Association (Card 2009), he presented a careful analysis of the potential role of immigration in explaining the increase in wage inequality from 1980 to 2005. By using the predicted fraction of immigrants in a community based on historical settlement patterns as an instrumental variable, he was able to avoid the bias that would result from the fact that immigrants tend to locate in areas with good labor markets and high wages. This approach then allowed Card to estimate the causal effect of increased immigration on relative wages in 124 large metropolitan areas. He concludes that immigration had very tiny effects on the college wage premium among native-born workers and that immigration could explain just 4% of the growth in this measure of wage inequality among all male workers and 6% of the increase among all female workers.

More recently, Eric Gould (2018) estimated the effects of the influx of low-skilled foreign-born workers on wage inequality among full-time prime-age native-born white workers, measured by their 90/10 wage ratio, across U.S. states and cities over the four decades from 1970 to 2000. His study is unique in examining the interaction of the decline in manufacturing employment, which can be traced to technological change and increased import competition and offshoring, and increased inflows of foreign-born workers with less than a college education on the market for workers in each state. An important conclusion is that, while increased immigration is found to increase the 90/10 wage ratio somewhat, the size of this effect depends on the simultaneous rate of decline of manufacturing employment in a state. A greater inflow of low-skill immigrants leads to a significantly larger increase in wage inequality among native-born workers in states that have lost more manufacturing jobs. This is consistent with the notion that the added supply of workers from immigration increased competition for and depressed wages in jobs in the low-wage service sector. Gould finds that the biggest increases in inequality were in states with both a relatively large increase in their immigrant population and a relatively large decline in manufacturing employment.

Based on this research, we might conclude that the wage inequality impact of increased immigration, in a manner similar to the effects of increased trade with low-income countries, depends critically on the broader economic situation prevailing in local labor markets. High rates of immigration appear to significantly worsen the negative effects of IT-driven automation and other aspects of globalization on wage and employment outcomes for low-skill U.S. workers.

4.5. Global Inequality

An interesting question is how the era of rapid globalization affected the distribution of wages among workers across the entire global economy. How did increased trade, outsourcing, new export opportunities and immigration affect the earnings of low-wage and high-wage workers? There is no single international data set with information on individual workers that could be used to estimate the global wage distribution at different points in time. However, resourceful scholars have attempted to overcome this limitation by merging survey and administrative data on individuals in different countries into worldwide data sets that permit the construction of measures of global inequality. Here, we take a brief look at the results of two such efforts reported in Lakner and Milanovic (2016) and Alvaredo *et al.* (2018). The construction of these data sets involves a number of methodological issues and assumptions that we cannot address in detail here.

Figure 4.6 illustrates how inflation-adjusted income, accounting for differences in the cost of living across countries, grew over the time periods examined in the two studies for individuals at different percentiles of the estimated global income distribution. Lakner and Milanovic (2016) base their estimates on income reported in household surveys for 63 countries with data for both of their reference years of 1988 and 2008. These 63 countries account for over 90% of the world GDP and include high-income economies as well as rapidly growing countries like China and India. Alvaredo *et al.* (2018) use surveys, tax returns and national accounts data to estimate the distribution of National Income within each country from 1980 to 2016. In pooling the country-specific data to construct a measure of global inequality, they assume that countries with missing data have the same distributions as other countries in the same region of the world. This allows them to characterize their results as estimates of the income distribution for the entire world economy.

Note that both of these studies use a broad measure that includes both labor and nonlabor sources of income. This is a deviation from our singular focus on wage inequality thus far in this section of the book. However, labor income is by far the largest share of total income for the vast majority of workers around the globe and these data are our only way of considering the worldwide distributional effects of globalization.

The graphs in Figure 4.6 have been dubbed "elephant curves" since they vaguely suggest the head of an elephant (to the left of the chart) with an upraised trunk (to the right). Although the two papers take quite distinct approaches to their estimates and cover different time periods, their

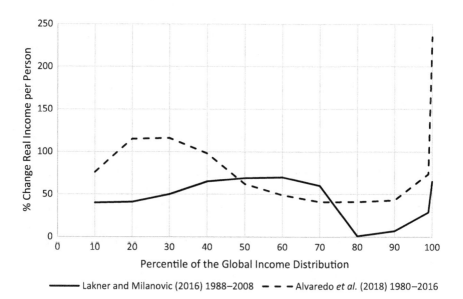

Figure 4.6:   Income Growth by Percentile of the Global Income Distribution

elephant curves suggest broadly similar conclusions about how globalization affected the worldwide distribution of income.

Looking first at the results from Lakner and Milanovic (2016), which
cover the period of increasing globalization, we see that real income grew
rapidly for those in the middle percentiles of the distribution, who largely
represent the middle class in Asia. Even workers at the 10th percentile
saw real incomes rise by 40% from 1988 to 2008. The suggestion of an
elephant comes in part from their estimate of very slow real income
growth at the 80th and 90th percentiles, which in the global distribution
include mainly middle- to low-income individuals in high-income countries like the U.S. Finally, their results show that income growth for the
middle percentiles of the distribution was even slightly faster than growth
for those in the top 1%, which is marked by the last point on the graph.
We have to remember that this chart shows the *growth* in income from
1988 to 2008 for those at different percentiles of the global income distribution. A small percentage increase in income for low-wage workers in
the U.S. can amount to a substantially greater increase in purchasing
power than a 70% increase for the "new middle class" in China or India.
Still, the elephant curve constructed by Lakner and Milanovic (2016)
clearly supports the conclusion that increased globalization largely benefited those with middle to low incomes on the global scale at the expense
of those with middle to low incomes in high-income economies.

The comprehensive attempt to estimate the income distribution for the
world economy by Alvaredo *et al.* (2018) reinforces this conclusion with
four slightly different results. First, their data cover a longer period and so
generate bigger cumulative percentage changes in real income at almost
every percentile of the distribution. Second, their curve has the elephant's
head further to the left, suggesting that the most rapid income growth
accrued to those below the global median income in comparison to those
in the 50th to 99th percentiles. Third, their estimates of income growth at
the 80th and 90th percentiles are substantially higher than that of Lakner
and Milanovic (2016), indicating perhaps a smaller cost imposed by globalization on middle- to low-income workers in high-income economies.
Finally, they find very rapid purchasing power growth for those in the top
1% of the distribution. We have discussed how surveys often underestimate the incomes of top earners, so the use of tax return data by Alvaredo
et al. may account for this difference between the two charts.

Both studies reach a similar conclusion – by these estimates, globalization significantly benefited middle- and low-wage workers in

low-income countries around the world. The growth of trade between low-income and high-income economies and the shift of manufacturing jobs to low-income economies through offshoring brought better employment opportunities to workers in places like China and India. As we have seen in our discussion of the wage inequality effects of globalization in this chapter, international trade, offshoring and, perhaps, immigration have not been so kind to low-wage workers in the United States and other high-income countries. While these workers are found in the top 20% of the estimated global income distribution, their real incomes increased the slowest from the 1980s to the first two decades of the 21st century. This development helps explain the virulent anti-globalization perspective of middle-income workers in the U.S. and Europe and the growing political aversion to international economic integration in recent years.

4.6. Summary

The long period of rising U.S. wage inequality overlaps the two decades from 1990 to the great recession when the integration of the global economy increased at its fastest pace since the years before World War I. Globalization had a number of effects on the wage differentials between high- and low-skill workers in America and other high-income economies.

The expansion of trade with low-income economies resulted in new market opportunities for U.S. exporters, who specialize in products and services produced by skilled labor. This expanded the demand for such workers, especially in finance and business services. On the other hand, U.S. manufacturing workers without college degrees faced heightened competition via imports from countries like China and India with abundant supplies of low-skill workers. These trade-induced shifts in labor market demand widened the wage differential between more highly educated and skilled workers and those with lower levels of skill. While economic theory still tends to emphasize long-run equilibrium, when market forces are expected to ameliorate the costs imposed on some from increased globalization, empirical evidence increasingly suggests that these costs persist for long periods of calendar time for affected workers and their communities.

Significant decreases in information and communication costs along with policy changes encouraged the development of global supply chains, with middle- and low-skill jobs shifted from the U.S. to overseas locations to take advantage of lower wages. The effect of offshoring in lowering production costs, thereby expanding sales and profits and the need for managers who could direct and monitor operations from afar, helped boost the demand for high-skill workers while jobs disappeared for middle-wage, routine-skill workers. Thus, offshoring reinforced the effect of automation in hollowing out the middle of the American wage distribution.

Both high- and low-skill foreign-born workers immigrated to the U.S. labor market in large numbers from 1970 to 2010. As a result, immigration was another factor increasing the gap between the wages earned and general employment opportunities available to high- and low-skill workers. By increasing labor supply, immigration of low-skill workers had negative effects on the earnings and employment opportunities of native-born workers without high school diplomas and previous cohorts of migrants. This impact was most pronounced in local labor markets adversely affected by the loss of manufacturing jobs. On the other hand, the growth in the number of highly educated foreign-born workers may have boosted the earnings of similarly educated natives. This is because high-skill immigrants increase the productivity of native-born workers and the profitability of their employers, outweighing their impact on the supply of high-skill workers.

There is some evidence that globalization had positive effects on the growth of income of workers at and below the median in the world distribution of income. Both of the global income inequality studies we examined show a decrease in the 90/10 income ratio during the period of enhanced global economic integration. This is consistent with the evidence of significant declines in the world poverty rate from 1990 until the onset of the COVID-19 pandemic. These gains appear to have come at the expense of medium and lower-skilled workers in the U.S. and other developed economies. While these workers are found at high percentiles of the world income distribution, their earnings increased at the slowest pace.

Many estimates of wage and employment effects from increased globalization are somewhat small in magnitude when examined at a national scale. This raises the possibility that the negative consequences of globalization are also small relative to our best guesses of the associated gains in economic efficiency. We have to be careful, however, in considering estimates of the quantitative effect of any single variable related to globalization. These estimates are derived from analyses that focus on a limited array of such variables. We have no attempts to estimate the combined quantitative effects of trade, offshoring, immigration and financial services exports on the U.S. wage distribution (see Helpman 2018). For our purposes, estimates of the size of the effect of any single variable are useful only to the extent that they provide evidence that the empirical results we are discussing are not trivial. The important conclusion is that globalization, along with technological change, has been a contributing factor to rising U.S. wage inequality.

Chapter 5

Institutional Changes

The effect of technological change and globalization on wage inequality is easily characterized as working through shifts in the demand and/or supply conditions prevailing in given labor markets. For example, since the U.S. and other high-income countries have a comparative advantage in high-skilled labor, an expansion of exports from the U.S. due to growth in international trade increases the demand for American workers with greater skills. On the other hand, the comparative advantage in low-skill labor in China and India means that an expansion of trade and increased import competition will have a negative effect on the demand for low-skill labor in the U.S. Thus, the market forces triggered by this one facet of increased globalization would be expected to widen the wage gap by skill in the U.S. and other high-income economies. Other globalization effects and the adoption of new technology in production would affect U.S. labor markets in a similar fashion.

In addition to shifts in labor demand and supply, it is important to consider the impact of institutions on labor market outcomes. By institutions, we mean the working rules or standard operating procedures followed by employers and workers in making decisions about employment or wages. These may be formal institutions, such as legal requirements regarding wages and hours or equal employment opportunity, practices prescribed by individual or collective bargaining contracts, and human resource management policies and procedures codified in employee handbooks. Or they may be informal working rules adopted in response to social norms and expectations or beliefs about the effectiveness of human resource management practices. An example might be a firm's commitment to promotion from within for certain jobs as a way of motivating worker effort.

Such institutions are particularly important in labor markets since both workers and firms typically expect the hiring transaction to establish a continuing employment relationship for some time and the transaction on the market is critically important to the well-being of employees and their families. This is still true even in the face of a growing "gig economy" where the employment relationship lasts only as long as it takes to complete a given task. Estimates of the size of the gig labor force by Abraham *et al.* (2019) indicate a very minor role for gig work outside the taxi industry which has come to be dominated by Uber in many large cities.

The role of institutions is also critical to understanding the unique aspects of American wage inequality. Technological change and globalization can explain why the 90/50 percentile wage ratio has risen over time. However, since the labor market effects of technology and global economic integration should be very similar in all high-income economies, they don't help us understand why the 90/50 wage ratio has been at a higher level and rising faster in the U.S. than in Europe. Changes in U.S. labor market institutions provide us with a country-specific set of inequality determinants.

The word "institution" connotes a sense of permanence and stability in the working rules and operating procedures affecting labor markets. In reality, institutions change and evolve with changes in public policy, changes in norms and expectations and changes in the organizational structure and managerial objectives of employers. The period of rising American wage inequality, which began in earnest during the 1980s, not only coincided with the rapid diffusion of digital technology and historic increases in globalization. It also coincided with a period of significant change in the factors shaping U.S. labor market institutions. The decades following the "Reagan-Thatcher revolution" of 1980 dramatically changed the public policy environment and norms of business behavior underlying U.S. labor market institutions.

These changes stemmed in large part from the political conflict associated with the Civil Rights Movement and the Vietnam War during the 1960s and the macroeconomic turmoil in the 1970s. This turmoil came from the abandonment of the Bretton-Woods fixed exchange rate system, the imposition of wage and price controls and two major oil price shocks at a time when the U.S. economy was heavily dependent on oil imports.

As a result, political power shifted to the Republican party, especially in the south, with its conservative pro-market and pro-business policy agenda and away from the Democratic party with its focus on a prominent role for the federal government in decreasing economic insecurity and promoting social justice that had prevailed since the Great Depression. In addition, the macroeconomic policy consensus shifted from an emphasis on using fiscal policy to achieve full employment to employing monetary policy to combat inflation. Finally, President Nixon's appointment of four conservative justices to the Supreme Court from 1968 to 1971 established a long-running conservative majority and resulted in a return to the court's traditional emphasis on protecting the private property rights of businesses and the freedom of contract between employers and employees when evaluating government laws and regulations.

How do these changes in the environment for labor market institutions affect wage inequality? We consider four factors that have been widely discussed in the recent literature that gives a prominent role to employer wage suppression policies in explaining wage inequality trends (Stansbury and Summers 2020; Taylor 2020).

First, there is growing recognition that real-world labor markets differ considerably from the purely competitive textbook model that views the firm as simply paying the "going wage" set by the market. Imperfect competition in product and labor markets, a diminished role for government regulation and increased employment risk facing workers all serve to enhance the bargaining power of employers who are wage setters.

Second, much has been made of the reduced frequency of federal minimum wage increases as a reflection of changes in U.S. labor policy. Over much of the post-1980 era, this has resulted in an erosion of the purchasing power of the minimum wage and its effectiveness as a low wage floor to the wage distribution.

Third, the research literature has focused on the impact of steadily falling rates of U.S. union membership and collective bargaining agreement coverage on wage inequality. Two defining actions of the Reagan-Thatcher revolution were President Reagan's firing of striking air traffic controllers in 1981 and Prime Minister Thatcher's defeat of the coal miner's strike in 1984–1985, both of which firmly established an anti-union bias to prevailing economic policy.

Fourth, we examine the way that increased managerial emphasis on cost-cutting to boost shareholder returns has affected wage inequality. Proponents of a shift to a more conservative stance toward labor market institutions argued effectively that the sole responsibility of business managers was to maximize profits. This perspective was reinforced by the deregulation of financial markets and rise to prominence of activist shareholders and private equity partnerships which dramatically focused managerial attention on profits, dividends and equity prices.

5.1. Imperfect Competition in Labor Markets

The model of a perfectly competitive labor market, one that has considerable influence in economic policy analysis, treats the firm as deciding on the size of the profit-maximizing workforce to hire given a going wage set by supply and demand in the relevant labor market. Supply and demand conditions in the markets for various types of labor are the focal point for an examination of factors leading to greater wage inequality in this model and there is limited scope for institutional determinants, especially those that might affect the wage policies of individual firms.

Yet it is very difficult to pin down the "going wage" for a given type of labor, other than for minimum wage jobs where the going wage is set by law rather than supply and demand. Instead of looking online or in the newspaper for information on the price of workers, like we do for the prices of commodities and financial assets, we typically use the average or median from a distribution of wages as a measure of the price of a given type of labor. Knowledge of the wage to be offered for filling a vacancy is often one of the last things applicants learn about a position. The labor market, then, fails the "law of one price" condition for purely competitive markets. In addition, research by Handwerker and Spletzer (2016) and Barth *et al.* (2016), among others, shows that much of the increase in wage inequality from the 1970s to the 2010s is due to a widening of wage differentials between business establishments both within and across industrial sectors. It appears that the wage policies of firms, in addition to supply and demand conditions, do indeed have a potentially important role to play in explaining rising wage inequality.

Recent theoretical developments have taken the economics of monopsony (a market with one buyer) beyond applications to isolated mining towns and a limited set of occupations to a general model of imperfect competition in labor markets. Imperfect competition would result from several factors (Manning 2021; Card 2022). Employers offer different sets of amenities, such as commuting time, working conditions and prestige, that provide additional value beyond monetary compensation to employees. In addition, employed and unemployed job searchers have limited information about the full range of alternative opportunities available to them in a relevant labor market and face substantial costs of continuing to search for a job. If I receive a job offer, I may not know what other offers I might yet get but it's costly to keep looking to find that out. In these models, firms are wage setters rather than wage takers and may have significant market power that translates into higher monetary returns.

One implication is that firms face an upward-sloping labor supply curve rather than the horizontal labor supply curve implied by pure competition. As a result, the firm can lower wages, or let real wages decline by keeping raises less than the rate of price inflation, without losing all or most of its workforce as it would in the case of a purely competitive market with complete information. The value of amenities, lack of information and costs of search would limit the number who might quit their jobs as real wages fell. The same factors, plus the fact that job searchers receive a limited number of offers in a given time period, could allow the firm to fill vacancies in its workforce at its current real wage even if other firms would offer a higher wage for similar work. However, in order to expand its workforce, the firm would have to increase the wage it offers to all workers.

The hypothesis that the firm's labor supply curve may be positively sloped provides an approach to empirically testing for the presence of imperfect labor market competition. This involves the estimation of the elasticity of labor supply to a firm. Elasticity in this case refers to the responsiveness of the quantity of labor supplied to a change in the wage and is measured by the percentage change in supply resulting from a wage change divided by the percentage change in the wage. In pure competition, it is assumed that labor supply is so highly responsive that an employer trying to offer a wage below the going amount would not be able to find workers willing to accept a job offer. In this case, the elasticity of labor supply to the firm would approach infinity.

Imperfect competition posits a much less wage-sensitive labor supply curve to the firm with the result that the firm's labor supply elasticity would be substantially less than infinity. And this is what most empirical studies of firm-specific labor supply curves tend to find. For example, Sokolova and Sorensen (2021) review this literature using the results of a meta-analysis of 1,320 separate estimates of the elasticity of the labor supply curve to individual firms from 53 research papers published between

1977 and 2019. While the estimates vary from study to study and vary for particular samples of firms, they are uniformly much less than infinity. Sokolova and Sorensen conclude that the "best practice" estimate of firm labor supply elasticity is 7.1, which implies that a 1% increase in the real wage offered by a firm would result in a 7.1% increase in its workforce, on average. Empirical estimates then support a key hypothesis from the theory of imperfect labor market competition.

A second implication is that the firm in an imperfectly competitive labor market can receive rent from exercising its market power in setting the wage. A rent in economics refers to a greater than normal profit (where a normal profit is the amount that is required to provide a sufficient return to the owners of the enterprise) that would not be competed away even over a long period of time. As Sokolova and Sorensen (2021) demonstrate, a profit-maximizing firm in an imperfectly competitive labor market would set its wage to hire enough workers on an upward-sloping labor supply curve so that

$$\text{Wage} = (\text{Marginal revenue product}) \times (\eta/1 + \eta) \qquad (5.1)$$

The marginal revenue product is the extra revenue received from selling the additional output the firm can produce with the help of the last worker hired. The elasticity of labor supply is η. In a competitive market, $\eta = \infty$, so the wage equals the marginal revenue product. If there is imperfect competition and, say, $\eta = 7.1$, then the wage will be equal to 0.88, or 88%, of the marginal revenue product. This leads to two conclusions: by paying a wage below the marginal revenue product, the firm can generate an economic rent, and the less elastic the supply curve (the smaller the η), the greater the power of the firm to set wages below the marginal revenue product.

Manning (2021) reviews a number of studies showing that firms that face less elastic labor supply curves do indeed pay lower wages as compared with estimates of their marginal revenue product. For example, a recent paper by Lamadon, Mostad and Setzler (2022) reports on a study of matched U.S. employer–employee data for 2001–2015. They find that, because of the value of amenities, the average worker would accept a 13% pay cut and still stay in her current job and the average firm earns rents amounting to 11% of its total profits. Additionally, Webber (2015) reports on research showing that increased firm market power, stemming from a less elastic firm labor supply curve, has a bigger negative effect on the wages of workers at lower percentiles of the firm's wage distribution, which would suggest that imperfect labor market competition would increase wage inequality.

There is some evidence that both the incidence of labor market monopsony (Benmelech, Bergman and Kim 2022) and the effects of monopsony on wages (Azar *et al.* 2020) have increased over the years during which the American wage distribution has become more dispersed. Additionally, Krueger (2018) points to growth over time in collusive practices, such as noncompete clauses, that limit the ability of a worker to move to another firm in the same industry, and no-poaching agreements, that prevent firms in the same labor market from hiring workers from competitors, as evidence of decreased labor market competition. Interestingly, in January 2023, the Federal Trade Commission proposed a new rule for public comment that would abolish noncompete agreements.[1] They cited the adverse impact of this practice on labor market competition and wage suppression as the rationale for the proposed new rule.

Equation (5.1) gives two additional insights into firm wage-setting behavior. If two firms have the same value for η, wages will be higher in the firm with a higher marginal revenue product. This would be a firm producing a product with a higher selling price and/or with a production process with greater worker productivity. Marginal revenue product differentials can be seen in an interesting recent study by Haltiwanger, Hyatt and Spletzer (2022). They found that much of the rise in between-firm wage dispersion from 1996 to 2018 stemmed from increased sorting of highly educated workers to firms in just 19 high-productivity, high-price industries, mainly in technology and finance. Increased employment of these workers came with significantly higher wages and salaries as suggested in Equation (5.1). They also found evidence of an increasing concentration of less-educated workers in firms in 11 low-productivity, low-price industries like restaurants and retail trade with only modest increases in wages.

In addition, Equation (5.1) identifies the lowest possible wage offer a firm could make, given the values for the marginal revenue product and labor supply elasticity, to maximize profits. Efficiency wage theory suggests that a firm might choose to offer a higher wage than this lowest possible wage, in effect sharing some portion of its current rents with its

---

[1] See https://www.ftc.gov/news-events/news/press-releases/2023/01/ftc-proposes-rule-ban-noncompete-clauses-which-hurt-workers-harm-competition.

workers. Firms that face a high cost of employee turnover because of their extensive investments in training and development might follow such a strategy to reduce quits. Or firms, where workers have some degree of control over their effort and monitoring costs are high, could use higher wages as an incentive for greater effort by increasing the potential cost of shirking if it is discovered. In addition to higher wages, efficiency wage concerns could lead the firm to provide nonwage amenities that are valued by its workers. The firm in essence is trading off higher wages today for greater worker productivity over the extent of the worker's tenure with the firm.

The theory of imperfect labor market competition would explain the widening of average wage differentials among individual firms, and the resulting increase in wage inequality, by the combined effect of a number of changes. One would be a widening of differences in product prices resulting from reduced product market competition and differing rates of new product development. Another would be increased variation in worker productivity among firms with differing capacities for boosting productivity through investment in equipment and technology. In addition, reductions in the elasticity of labor supply to some firms, from reduced labor market competition and greater worker uncertainty about alternative job opportunities, would add to wage variation among firms. Finally, changes in turnover and monitoring costs would also play a role.

It's important to note that the existence of rents stemming from the firm's ability to pay wages less than the marginal revenue product of workers means that workers with individual or collective bargaining power could negotiate a higher wage or the government could mandate a higher minimum wage without affecting the level of employment at the firm or its normal profit as long as the resulting wage was at least equal to or less than the marginal revenue product of the firm. However, such offsets to employer bargaining power have waned over the years.

5.2. Minimum Wages

Under the Fair Labor Standards Act of 1938, the U.S. Congress sets a minimum hourly wage rate for the vast majority of workers. The federal minimum wage is set in nominal terms rather than being linked to the cost of living or, as in many European countries, to the median wage among all workers. Changes in the federal minimum wage are contentious political issues and, as a result, are infrequently enacted. The federal minimum wage of $7.25 an hour prevailing in 2023 was first set at that amount in July 2009. State legislatures and some city governments have the power to supersede the federal minimum wage by establishing their own minimum wage levels. In 2022, 28 states plus the District of Columbia (DC) had legislated higher minimum wages with the highest hourly levels in DC at $15.20, Massachusetts (MA) at $14.25 and California (CA) at $14.00. This represents a sharp increase from 2000 when just 9 states and DC set minimum wages higher than the federal level. In another recent development, 39 localities, mostly in CA, legislated 2022 minimum wage levels for their jurisdictions that exceeded both the prevailing federal and state minimums.[2]

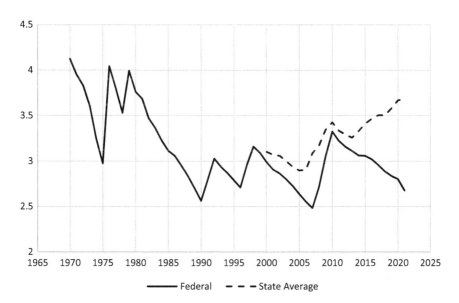

Figure 5.1: The Real U.S. Minimum Wage

Source: Data on the Federal and State Minimum Wage levels are from the FRED database maintained by the Federal Reserve Bank of St. Louis accessed at https://fred.stlouisfed.org/. Nominal minimum wages are deflated by the Consumer Price Index for all Urban Consumers (1982–84 = 100) available at https://bls.gov.

---

[2]See the Economic Policy Institute Minimum Wage Tracker at https://www.epi.org/minimum-wage-tracker/.

Figure 5.1 traces the evolution of the real federal minimum wage, adjusted for changes in the consumer price index for all urban consumers, over the period from 1970 to 2022. The sawtooth pattern of the time series reflects the fact that minimum wages are set in nominal terms that remain unchanged for a period of years. So, for example, over the years since 2010, the real federal minimum wage declined by nearly 20% because consumer price inflation steadily eroded the purchasing power of the $7.25 minimum required by law.

The time series pattern of the real minimum wage demonstrates a significant downward shift following the economic policy changes after 1980. During the decade of the 1970s, the real federal minimum wage fluctuated between $3 and $4 per hour, averaging $3.71 during that period. Big increases in 1976 and 1979 were able to offset the impact of rapidly rising consumer prices. From 1979 to 1990, the real federal minimum wage fell steadily, dropping by 36%. And from 1990 to 2021, the real federal minimum wage ranged between $2.50 and $3.32 per hour, averaging $2.89. The time series in Figure 5.1 provides visual evidence of a shift to a lower level for the real minimum wage after 1980.

Figure 5.1 also presents an alternative estimate of the real U.S. minimum wage for the years since 2000. This is the average of the minimum wage prevailing in each state, either the federal minimum or a higher minimum legislated by the state, weighted by the state's share of total nonfarm employment. The annual weighted average state minimum wage is also adjusted for inflation by deflating nominal values by the consumer price index for all urban consumers. The number of states with separate minimum wage requirements has increased since 2000 and many have made frequent adjustments to their minimum wage or linked their minimums to inflation. As a result, the time series pattern of the real average state minimum wage looks very different from the federal minimum wage, especially since 2010. Instead of falling like the real federal minimum wage, its value grew by about 8% from 2010 to 2021. Of course, this comes with a widening spread in the prevailing real minimum wage between those states requiring the federal minimum and those with separate legislated amounts. For example, the neighboring states of Pennsylvania (PA) and New York (NY) had the same real minimum wage in 2010 but by 2021 the NY minimum exceeded the PA minimum by 82%.

Figure 5.2 provides a dramatic illustration of the way in which a minimum wage can affect the distribution of wages. The data charted there are for U.K. hourly earnings for all workers 16 years of age and older for

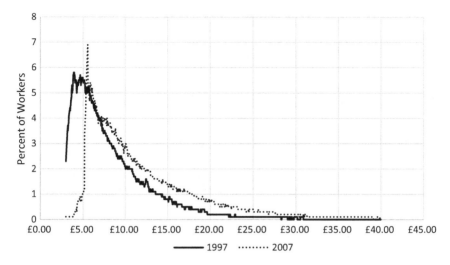

Figure 5.2:   The Distribution of Hourly Earnings in the U.K., 1997 and 2007

Source: https://www.ons.gov.uk/employmentandlabourmarket/peopleinwork/earningsandworking
hours/articles/analysisofthedistributionofearningsacrosstheukusingashedata/2016.

1997 and 2007. In order to generate smoother graphs, each point on the curves shows the percentage of workers receiving that rate of hourly pay plus and minus 20 cents. As a result of using this rolling sum of the density of workers in each pay bracket, the cumulative distribution won't add to 100%. However, we can still see the effect of the adoption of a national minimum wage on the distribution of wages.

The distribution for 1997 follows the typical pattern we expect from wage distributions with a large concentration of earners at the low end of the pay scale and a long right tail, indicating that a very small percentage of workers earn very high hourly wages. There was no national minimum wage in the U.K. in 1997. The wage distribution for 2007 looks quite a bit different with a big spike near the national minimum wage of £5.35 in place for that year. The minimum wage can be seen as creating a floor for the wage distribution with the density of workers earning less than £5 dramatically lower, and near zero, in 2007 than in 1997. In contrast, the distribution of wages above the minimum wage in 2007 resembles closely the distribution in 1997 although it is shifted to the right a bit as a result of inflation and productivity growth.

Several recent studies provide econometric support for the conclusion that changes in minimum wage policy played an important role in the post-1980 evolution of wage inequality, especially for those earning less than the median wage. These studies take advantage of differences in minimum wage levels across U.S. states to identify the policy effect on the wage distribution and typically define the policy variable as the effective minimum wage prevailing in a particular state and time period. The effective minimum wage is usually defined as the statutory minimum wage divided by the median wage. This definition is based on the assumption that a given minimum wage level will have a bigger effect in labor markets with a lower median wage. In the statistical analysis, the legislated minimum wage is used as an instrumental variable for the effective minimum wage, allowing for a causal interpretation of the link between the minimum wage and inequality.

Autor, Manning and Smith (2016) discover a statistically significant negative relationship between the effective minimum wage and the 50/10 percentile wage ratio, particularly for female workers and for the decade of the 1980s, in a sample of U.S. employees aged 16–64. The decrease in the value of the effective minimum wage from 1979 to 2012 can account for about half of the increased lower tail wage inequality for women and around 10% of the increase in the male 50/10 ratio. They also find evidence for substantial spillover effects by which an increase in the effective minimum wage raises wages for those slightly above the minimum.

Fortin, Lemieux and Lloyd (2021) explore spillover effects further using an innovative statistical technique, distribution regressions, to estimate the impact of the effective minimum wage at different points in the wage distribution. Their main conclusion is that the observed decrease in the effective minimum wage can account for most of the increase in the 50/10 percentile wage differential during the 1980s. They also conclude that a rise in the effective minimum wage, as suggested by the increase in the state average minimum displayed in Figure 5.1, helps explain the slight decrease in the 50/10 percentile differential in the years after 2010. Their results also indicate that a minimum wage increase would sharply lower the fraction of workers earning less than the minimum and increase the share with wages at or slightly above the minimum wage.

Additional empirical evidence is provided by Joe and Moon (2020) who estimate minimum wage effects using aggregate data for 27 OECD countries over the period from 1990 to 2017. They find that a 1% increase in the effective minimum wage was associated with a 0.09% reduction in the 50/10 wage ratio for men and a 0.19% reduction in the 50/10 wage ratio for women. Like the previous two studies, there is no evidence in their work for a statistically significant impact of the effective minimum wage on either the 90/50 or 90/10 percentile differentials. The impact of a higher minimum wage on inequality seems limited to reducing inequality at the lower tail of the wage distribution with larger effects for women than men.

Finally, we return to the issue of a growing gap between states where the federal minimum wage is mandated and states that have a minimum wage that exceeds the federal level and the impact of this on wage inequality. Figure 5.3 plots a scatter diagram linking the percentage change in the state minimum wage minus the percentage change in the Federal minimum wage to the percentage change in the 50/10 wage ratio from 2001 to 2019 for each of the 50 states. Among the 22 states mandating the federal minimum wage, stacked up at zero on the *x*-axis in Figure 5.3, only Idaho experienced a decrease in the lower tail wage inequality from 2001 to 2019. The average percentage change in the 50/10 wage ratio for these 22 states is 5.21%. By contrast, 19 of the 28 states

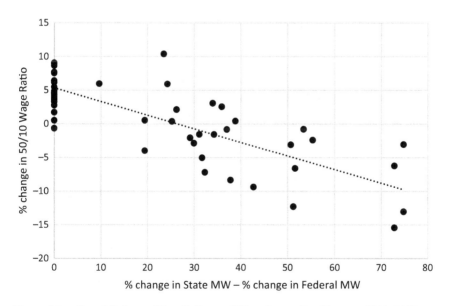

Figure 5.3:   State Minimum Wage Policy and Wage Inequality Changes, 2001–2019

Source: See the footnote to Figure 5.1 for the source of minimum wage data. Data on the 50/10 wage ratio for the 50 states are from the Occupational Employment and Wage Statistics at https://www.bls.gov/oes/.

legislating minimum wage requirements above the federal level saw their 50/10 wage ratios decrease from 2001 to 2019. The average of the 2001–2019 percentage change in the 50/10 wage ratio for these 28 states is –2.65%.

The scatter plot in Figure 5.3 clearly demonstrates a negative relationship across the 50 states between the growth or decline in lower tail wage inequality and the growth in the gap between state and federal minimum wage levels. The slope of the trend line indicates that a ten-point difference in the growth of this gap is associated with a two-point decrease in the growth of the 50/10 wage ratio. While correlation is not causation, it is of interest to note that the trend line plotted in Figure 5.3 also indicates that variation in the percentage change in the state minimum relative to the percentage change in the Federal level is able to "explain" more than 60% of the variation in the percentage change in the 50/10 wage ratio. The data in Figure 5.3 are consistent with more careful econometric studies of the impact of minimum wage policy on lower tail inequality. And, like the results reported by Fortin, Lemieux and Lloyd (2021), the figure suggests that the increase since 2000 in the number of states adopting minimum wages that exceed the federal level may have been a significant factor in the observed post-2010 decrease in the U.S. 50/10 wage ratio.

5.3. Unions and Collective Bargaining Agreements

In his best-selling book, *The New Industrial State*, John Kenneth Galbraith (1967) argued that unions, along with the government, were an important countervailing power to the growing economic influence of large U.S. corporations. However, by the publication date of his book, the strength of the union movement had already passed its peak and begun the long steady decrease that has extended to this day.

Figure 5.4 documents this decline, presenting data from the nationally representative Current Population Survey (CPS) on union density (see Hirsch and McPherson 2003), defined as the percentage of U.S. workers who identified themselves as union members, over the period 1973–2020. There is a sharp distinction evident between the trends in union density in the public and private sectors. After growing rapidly in the 1970s due to the passage of numerous state laws permitting collective bargaining for state and local employees, union members as a percentage of public sector

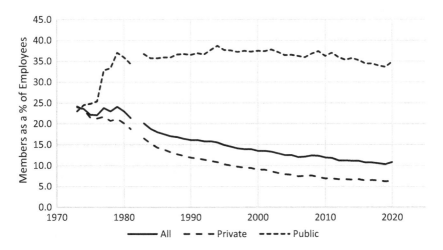

Figure 5.4: U.S. Union Density 1973–2020

Source: See the detailed description in Hirsch and McPherson (2003). Data are updated regularly and available at https://unionstats.com/. Data for 1973 to 1981 are from the May CPS while that for 1983 to the present are from the CPS Outgoing Rotation Group files. No data are available for 1982.

employment remained fairly constant before declining slightly after 2010. By contrast, private sector union density has declined steadily from 20.1% of private sector workers in 1973 to 6.3% in 2020. Private sector union density decreased most rapidly during the decade of the 1980s, falling by 8.2 percentage points from 1980 to 1990. From 1990 to 2020, density fell by an additional 5.6 percentage points over those three decades. Because private sector employment greatly exceeds the number of public sector workers, the trend in union density for all workers closely followed that for private sector workers.

An alternative measure of union strength is the percentage of workers covered by collective bargaining agreements. Because contracts cover all workers in a bargaining unit, whether or not they are union members, the union contract coverage rate is slightly higher than the union density rates plotted in Figure 5.4. From 1980 to 2020, union contract coverage fell from 43.4% to 38.4% of public sector workers and from 21.7% to 7.2% of private sector workers. The decline in union density and contract coverage is matched by data on union militancy. The number of work stoppages involving 1,000 employees or more averaged 308 per year from 1950 to

1979.[3] This dropped to 59 per year on average from 1980 to 1999 and just 18 per year from 2000 to 2019.

The decline in U.S. private sector unionization has been attributed to a shift in jobs away from traditional union strongholds in goods production sectors and the industrial northeast and a shift in national policy to a negative perspective on unions after the inflationary spiral of the 1970s and President Reagan's reaction to the strike by air traffic controllers. In addition, a stronger and more sophisticated management response to union organizing efforts, abetted by weak sanctions on illegal employer tactics and a shift of dwindling union resources from organizing new members to servicing ongoing members, also contributed to the trend in private sector union density shown in Figure 5.4 (Farber and Western 2001; Fiorito 2007; Godard 2009).

Evidence of the declining fortunes of American labor unions is relevant to this chapter's theme because a large literature has found that a higher union density in the workforce is linked to greater wage equality. In fact, my first publication in an influential journal (Hyclak 1979) provided evidence that the percentage of workers covered by union contracts was negatively correlated with earnings inequality among all male and black male workers, but not all female and black female workers, across metropolitan labor markets in 1970. This gender difference in the link between inequality and unions has been a common finding of more recent studies. The equalizing effect of unions can be traced to union wage bargains that focus on dollar-per-hour wage increases that amount to larger percentage gains for the lowest-paid workers. Also important is the spillover of union wage policies to nonunion establishments, who view paying near-union wages as an effective way of forestalling the organization of their employees. Rather than trying to review the entire empirical literature on this question, I focus on three recent studies that reinforce the conclusion that collective bargaining is an important institutional determinant of inequality and that go beyond correlation to establish a potentially causal effect of declining unionization on the increase in American wage inequality since 1980.

First, Card, Lemieux and Riddell (2020) re-examine the union–inequality relationship taking into account the huge change over time in the composition of union membership. By 2015, around half of the union members were public sector employees and nearly half were women.

---

[3] Data are available at https://www.bls.gov/web/wkstp/annual-listing.htm.

They compare U.S. outcomes with those in Canada, which has a similar collective bargaining system but which has experienced a smaller decrease in union density and a smaller increase in wage inequality over time. Their method is to compare the statistical variance in hourly wages in a given period with an estimated counterfactual variance that would exist in the absence of unions. The critical assumption is that the actual variance among nonunion workers is an accurate predictor of the wage variance that would prevail in an economy without any unions at all.

For U.S. workers, they find that greater union density was associated with reduced inequality with this equalizing effect larger in the public sector, declining over time in both the private and public sectors and somewhat similar among men and women in 2015. For example, in 1984, union membership is estimated to have reduced the wage variance among U.S. men by 4% in the private sector and 19.6% in the public sector. For 2015, the estimates are 1.7% in the private sector and 16.2% in the public sector. In 2015, union density is estimated to have reduced the wage variance for women by 0.6% in the private sector and 10.7% in the public sector.

Among Canadian workers, the estimated effects of union membership on male and female hourly wage inequality were broadly similar to those found for U.S. workers. However, the union impact on Canadian public sector employees was much bigger and equal for men and women. In 1984, Canadian unions are estimated to have reduced the wage variance among both male and female public sector workers by about 71% while by 2015 union membership is found to lower the variance among men and women by 50%. Card, Lemieux and Riddell (2020) reinforce the conclusion common to many studies that the extent of union activity is associated with greater wage equality and that this is an association that has declined in strength along with the union movement over the past four decades. They add significantly to the literature by their finding that gender differences in the union impact have moderated over time and mainly reflect gender differences in employment between the public and private sectors.

Second, Farber, Herbst and Kuziemko (2021) develop a new time series of data on union membership going back to 1936 from nearly a million individual survey responses to the Gallup poll and other household surveys. Prior to their efforts, the only union membership data based on surveys was the CPS data beginning in 1973 that are presented in Figure 5.4. Membership data exist for earlier periods but are based on union administrative records that are not considered to be fully accurate. This new data source allows them to examine the effect of union membership density on wage inequality during the period when membership was expanding as well as during the years when union density has been steadily falling.

There are three main conclusions from their research. First, the rapid growth of union membership in the late 1930s and 1940s was spurred by supportive federal policy embodied in the Wagner Act of 1935 and the decisions of the federal War Labor Board, established to ensure labor peace during World War II. Second, households with union members had labor earnings that were 10–20% higher than nonunion households with larger union wage premiums in nonwhite households and those with less education. Finally, they find strong evidence that union density was an important determinant of wage inequality. In regressions on state-level data that control for state and year effects, the *increase* in union density from 1936 to 1968 is estimated to explain 14–17% of the *decrease* in the Gini coefficient of family income during the same period while 12–15% of the *rise* in the Gini coefficient from 1986 to 2014 is attributed to the corresponding *decrease* in union density.

Third, Fortin, Lemieux and Lloyd (2021) examine the effects of both union density and minimum wages on wage inequality, using an advanced statistical technique that allows them to capture the spillover effects of both institutional variables. They find that, within narrowly defined industries, unionization is positively correlated with the wage level of nonunion workers. The strength of this union spillover effect has weakened over time in their estimates but remains significant in recent years. They also find that a higher minimum wage significantly increased the probability that a worker would earn a wage that was above the minimum wage level. This minimum wage spillover effect extended to those earning as much as 30% more than the minimum wage in the 1979–1988 period and 20% more in later years.

These spillover effects enhanced their estimated effect of union density and the level of the minimum wage on wage inequality. For men, the decline in union density from 1979 to 2017, taking spillovers into account, is estimated to explain as much as 27% of the increase in the 90/10 percentile wage ratio over that time span. This is about twice the estimated effect of unionization without spillovers. For men, the combined effect of declining union density and real minimum wage levels, including spillover effects, from 1979 to 2017 can account for nearly 60% of the increase in the 90/10 ratio over this period. For women, the combined effect of union density and the real minimum wage plus spillovers is estimated to explain about 27% of the 1979 to 2017 increase in the 90/10 percentile wage ratio. It is evident that decreases since the 1970s in these two institutional variables have a significant role to play in explaining the rise in U.S. wage inequality over the last forty years.

5.4. The Fissured Workplace

David Weil (2014) coined this term to describe the effect of domestic outsourcing on the wage structure of large American corporations. Domestic outsourcing refers to the process by which jobs that once were filled by employees of the firm are shifted to the employees of contractors who provide services to the firm under detailed specifications and close supervision. Such shifting of jobs has involved white-collar functions such as payroll, accounting, customer service and some aspects of human resource management and blue-collar functions such as janitorial services, maintenance, security and fulfillment of online retail orders. Note that this involves a different organizational change than automation or global supply chains. In this case, the work remains at the firm; it is not replaced by computers and machines nor is it shifted abroad. However, the work is done by employees of a contractor rather than employees of the firm itself.

A primary motivation to outsource jobs in this manner, according to Weil, has been the effort to improve performance and increase shareholder returns by concentrating on managing the workforce engaged in core activities. There are also savings involved in shifting pay, hours and benefit administration and regulatory compliance for affected workers to the contractor. Finally, competition among potential contractors and the bargaining power of the firm in negotiating the price of services can substantially lower the cost to the firm of outsourced functions.

The term "fissuring" refers to the effect of such outsourcing on the wage structure of the firm. Most large firms have internal labor markets where workers are generally hired into entry-level positions in a job hierarchy and can move up the job ladder as vacancies become available with the firm generally filling higher-level positions by promotion from within. This provides workers with the incentive to stay with the firm and exert the effort needed to gain promotion. Because workers are concerned about horizontal equity in relative pay across the various job hierarchies within the firm and vertical equity among those in a given hierarchy, the relative pay structure of jobs within the firm is set and maintained somewhat independently of developments in the external labor market. Back in the day, clerical jobs at Bethlehem Steel were seen as very good jobs because they paid higher wages and benefits than those that were prevalent for clerical workers in the local labor market. Outsourcing jobs is a way of breaking the structure of relative wages within the internal labor market without significantly affecting the incentives or fairness concerns of remaining employees.

The fissured workplace could contribute to rising wage inequality if those working for contract firms accounted for a growing share of the overall workforce and earned lower wages than similar workers employed directly by producers. The BLS periodically asks about contingent and alternative work arrangements as part of the CPS. One category of such arrangements are workers provided by contract firms. These are defined as workers whose employer provides them or their services to others under contract, who are usually assigned to only one customer and who usually work at the customer's worksite.[4] The results of the latest survey in 2017 showed that 0.6% of all workers were provided by contract firms and that the relative importance of contract workers changed little from 1995 to 2017. This would suggest a small role for fissuring in rising wage inequality.

However, the accuracy of these data has been questioned because many workers apparently aren't aware that they are contract workers and the member of the household who responds to a survey may not know about the contract status of other household members. Katz and Krueger (2019) attempt to refine the BLS data by taking into account tax information, other survey information, the level of unemployment and whether the identified work arrangement was that of the respondent to the survey or some other household member. Their revision raises the percentage of contract workers a bit to 1.4% in 2017 up slightly from 1.3% in 1995.

The relative importance of contract work differs substantially among occupations, with janitors and security guards among the workers most affected. Dube and Kaplan (2010) study these two occupations, defining contract janitors as those who were employed in the services to buildings

---

[4]See the BLS News Release "Contingent and Alternative Employment Arrangements – May 2017" available at https://www.bls.gov/news.release/pdf/conemp.pdf.

and dwellings industry and security guards as those employed in the protective services industry. They find that the percentage of janitors who were contract workers rose from 16% in the early 1980s to nearly 22% by 2000 while the number of contract workers as a percentage of security guards rose from 40% to 50% over the same time frame. Controlling for personal and industry characteristics, they also find evidence of a substantial wage penalty of 4–7% for contract janitors and 8–24% for contract security guards. For these occupations, Dube and Kaplan (2010) conclude that domestic outsourcing raised wage inequality by shifting workers from higher-paid jobs with employers sharing rents from imperfect competition to lower-paid jobs with contractors in a more competitive economic environment.

Table 5.1 describes developments in the market for janitors and cleaners for the period after 2000, using Occupational Employment and Wage Statistics data from the BLS. As in Dube and Kaplan (2010), contract janitors are defined as those working in the services to buildings and dwellings industry. Unfortunately, this BLS data source does not provide information on the protective services industry so we cannot extend the post-2000 analysis to security guards.

In 2002, 32% of all janitors and cleaners were thus identified as contract workers. From 2002 to 2019, the fraction of jobs accounted for by contract janitors rose to 41% with the number of contract workers rising by 226,290 while the number of janitors and cleaners in noncontract positions fell by 132,930. Clearly, the shift to contract work in this occupation continued apace after 2000. Table 5.1 also indicates that average hourly

Table 5.1: Workplace Fissuring for Janitors and Cleaners, 2002–2019

	Employment	Average Hourly Wage ($)
May 2002		
Contract	657,070	8.35
Noncontract	1,395,020	10.32
May 2019		
Contract	883,360	13.43
Noncontract	1,262,090	15.13

Source: Author's calculations from Occupational Employment and Wage Statistics data at www.bls.gov/oes/tables.htm. Contract workers are those employed in the services to buildings and dwellings industry.

earnings for contract janitors were lower than the average hourly earnings for noncontract janitors by 23.5% in 2002 and 12.7% in 2019. Note, however, that these are "raw" wage comparisons with no adjustment for differences in personal and industry wage determinants between the two groups. Still, the results reported in Table 5.1 are consistent with those found by Dube and Kaplan (2010) that contracting out for the work done by janitors and cleaners increased over time and that contract employees earned significantly lower wages than noncontract janitors and cleaners.

An interesting study by Goldschmidt and Schmieder (2017) uses German social security records to track food preparation, cleaning, security and logistics workers who found themselves shifted from noncontract jobs to employment with business services or temporary help agencies. The percentage of workers in these occupations who were employed by contract services firms rose from around 2% in 1975 to 7% in 2009 and workers who were moved to these firms experienced a 10–15% drop, most likely from slower wage growth, in their wages relative to workers who continued to hold traditional jobs that were not outsourced. Goldschmidt and Schmieder (2017) estimate that outsourcing food, cleaning, security and logistics could account for as much as 9% of the increase in German wage inequality from 1975 to 2009.

This small number of empirical studies tends to support Weil's (2014) argument that domestic outsourcing was a potentially important determinant of rising U.S. wage inequality after 1980. It is difficult to clearly identify contract workers in widely used data sets and this has limited empirical studies to the examination of outcomes for a few occupations that account for a small fraction of overall employment. As a result, we are unsure of the overall scope of the impact of outsourcing on inequality. However, the strength of the employment and wage results for janitors and security guards and the fairly large number of white- and blue-collar occupations that have been subjects of outsourcing suggest that fissuring might well be a more significant factor than we have been able to determine thus far.

5.5. Summary

A significant shift in the institutional framework of U.S. labor markets coincided with the period of rising wage inequality. Federal government policy, and that of many states, turned firmly toward a pro-business, pro-market, anti-union direction. A similar shift can be seen in the philosophical makeup of the Supreme Court as the liberal Earl Warren court was replaced in 1969 by the conservative Warren Burger court and subsequently the William Rehnquist and John Roberts courts. And norms of managerial behavior shifted away from some concern for the well-being of employees and communities to a fairly single-minded focus on delivering shareholder value. This was reinforced by financial market deregulation and the growing influence of activist investors and private equity firms, which acquire underperforming businesses, restructure them and sell the competitive pieces in public offerings or private placements.

To examine the effect of institutional changes on the labor market, economists have increasingly turned to models of imperfect competition in which firms are wage setters rather than wage takers. In such models, firms enjoy bargaining power stemming from informational asymmetries, significant job search and job switching costs, and preferences for various amenities among workers. In response to the institutional changes described above, firms would have a greater incentive to use their bargaining power more fully to lower wages and boost profits directly by outsourcing the employment of workers in certain positions. There is some empirical evidence that the extent of imperfect competition has increased, that wages are more responsive to firm bargaining power and that outsourcing has increased over time and lowered the wages of outsourced workers. This would lead us to conclude that institutional change has contributed to rising wage inequality and help explain the finding that increased disparity across firms is a primary source of inequality. However, difficulties in measuring the degree of labor market monopsony, the extent of firm bargaining power and the rate of outsourcing cloud our ability to assess the strength of these changes.

Worker bargaining power, buttressed by government policy and typically expressed through collective bargaining, is seen as the main offset to the bargaining power of the firm. Here measurement is relatively easy and there is strong empirical evidence that higher real or relative minimum wages and higher rates of unionization are associated with greater wage equality. The lower average value of the real federal minimum wage and the steady decline in union membership and contract coverage since 1980 have played significant roles in the rise of wage inequality since then. An important caveat to that conclusion is that the number of states requiring higher minimum wages than the federal level has increased substantially since 2000. The impact of higher state-federal minimum wage differences may be an important determinant of the rise in the 10th percentile wage level since 2010.

Since we are ending our coverage of the causes of rising wage inequality here, it might be of value to recap what we have learned. There are, in my estimation, five major takeaways from Chapters 2–4 to add to the conclusions about institutions outlined above:

First, the skilled wage differential reflects the outcome of a race between technological change, which boosts the demand for those with more skills or education, and the supply of workers with the requisite skill or education. In the 1970s, when the supply of college-educated people increased faster than the demand, the college-high school wage differential fell. After 1980, the technology-fueled demand for college-educated workers grew faster than the supply, which actually fell over some periods, and the college-high school wage differential rose steadily. The dissemination of digital technology and the resulting rise in the college-high school wage ratio are seen as the main factor behind rising U.S. wage inequality during the 1980s and 1990s.

Second, the wage inequality impact of technological change also reflects the ability of digital equipment to replace jobs through automation. The potential for this is, at least initially, highest in jobs requiring routine, manual skills since these jobs can be more readily programmed than those requiring cognitive or nonmanual skills. However, artificial intelligence may well expand the possibilities of automating cognitive and nonmanual jobs in the future. The result has been a hollowing out of the wage distribution with middle-wage jobs declining while high- and low-wage jobs increase with economic growth. This type of automation helps explain the stagnant time series of median wages and, for the years after 2010, the noticeable shrinkage of the 50/10 percentile wage ratio.

Third, the U.S. economy, which has had a chronic trade deficit since the 1970s, faced a major foreign trade shock in the decade or so following the turn of the 21st century. Trade with less developed economies, in particular with China, expanded rapidly and many localities with industry mixes heavily weighted toward sectors susceptible to import competition suffered significant decreases in manufacturing employment and average wage levels. The negative consequences for local labor markets subject to this China Shock extended to the housing market and the reliance of the population on various forms of government support. The nation as a whole experienced widening wage inequality as geographic differentials increased and manufacturing employment fell substantially. The negative consequences also persisted until 2019, almost a full decade after the shock itself dissipated, with no signs of an adjustment to a new equilibrium.

Fourth, the opening of China and other low-wage countries to foreign direct investment and the drop in shipping and communication costs made feasible global supply chains that separated product development, production and marketing into functions that could be carried out in different countries thousands of miles apart. Again, routine manual jobs that could be specified in great detail and monitored by IT were more susceptible to offshoring to low-wage countries. So, job polarization or hollowing out of the wage distribution was fostered both by automation and offshoring.

Fifth, globalization presented other opportunities for U.S. firms. Firms producing with high-skill labor saw export opportunities expand and, as a result, hired more high-skill workers and bid up their wages. In particular, the U.S. trade deficit increased the dollar holdings of foreigners which led to an increased desire to invest in U.S. financial assets and to an export of financial services by U.S. institutions. This added to the expansion of the U.S. financial services sector which has always employed a large share of highly educated and highly paid workers. Finally, offshoring also contributed to a rise in the wages of well-paid individuals who could effectively manage and keep connected to a far-flung global supply chain. The current shorthand assessment seems to be that tech was the primary determinant of rising wage inequality from 1980 to 2000, after which globalization became the main factor driving skill differentials and inequality higher.

We turn our attention in the final two chapters to a consideration of inequality in the ownership of financial and real assets that constitute the wealth of the U.S. and to an examination of the pre- and post-tax and transfer distribution of income from labor and nonlabor sources among U.S. households. The last chapter summarizes the main arguments concerning the consequences of high and rising inequality and presents policy options for reducing inequality should society choose to pursue that path.

Chapter 6

Wealth and Income Inequality

We now turn our attention away from the manner in which labor market developments have affected disparities in the wages and salaries paid to individual workers to an examination of inequality in the wealth and total income of households. Households are defined as individuals residing alone or living together, whether or not they are members of the same family. Since households share resources, engage in joint consumption spending and include children and the elderly who are not in the work-force, these are natural units to examine in evaluating changes over time in the standard of living of the population.

Wealth and income are related measures of the standard of living of household units. Wealth is measured by the stock of assets owned by a household, including real assets such as real estate and businesses and financial assets such as stocks and bonds, minus the total debt owed by the household at a given point in time. This measure of wealth, also referred to as the household's net worth, adds up the cumulative savings of the household over time and represents the resources available to fund major expenditures, such as meeting living expenses in retirement. Total income from economic activity is measured by the household's annual receipt of wages and salaries from labor and the rent, profits, interest, dividends and capital gains that flow from the ownership of real and financial assets. In order to fully represent the resources available to meet the ongoing consumption needs of the household, we also have to adjust the total income for the taxes paid and payments received from the government. Thus, wealth and income are alternative ways of measuring how "rich" someone is or, to use the language of economics, how high is their standard of living.

It is very important to be clear about the distinction between an income flow and the value of an asset when we consider wealth and income inequality. For example, the ownership of a share of corporate stock represents an asset that is a claim on the profits of the corporation. Profits are shared through the payment of periodic cash dividends to the shareholders. These dividend payments are a flow of income to the recipient and must be declared on income tax returns. The value of the shares owned by the recipient is not income, and thus not subject to income tax, but rather is a part of the recipient's net worth (assets minus debt and other liabilities) or wealth on the household's balance sheet. In addition to asset-related income flows from dividends, interest, rent and proprietor's income, an asset owner also realizes cash income when an asset is sold for a higher price than was paid for it. Such capital gains are also subject to income tax.

Of course, the distributions of wages, income and wealth are interconnected. While the compensation of workers as a share of income generated in the U.S. nonfarm business sector has fallen from around 65% in the late 1990s to 58% in the mid-2010s (Giandrea and Sprague 2017), wages and salaries remain the largest source of total income for the vast majority of households. So, it would be surprising if the steady rise in wage inequality that we have examined in previous chapters wasn't also reflected in the distribution of pre-tax and pre-transfer total income. An interesting question is the extent to which government tax and transfer programs offset rising inequality in earned income.

In addition to wages and salaries, total household income includes the receipt of rent, profits, interest and dividends from the ownership of wealth. Households who own more wealth will receive a greater flow of such nonlabor income in each time period and inequality in the distribution of wealth will contribute to inequality in the distribution of household income. During the Gilded Age at the turn of the 20th century, the Astors, Rockefellers and Vanderbilts enjoyed a luxurious standard of living largely from the receipt of nonlabor income generated by their vast holdings of real and financial assets. At the same time, households accumulate wealth by allocating a portion of their total income to saving instead of consumption. Those with higher incomes generally save a higher fraction of their total income, so greater income inequality will contribute to inequality in the distribution of wealth. Our current age of inequality differs from the Gilded Age in that the richest households enjoy both very high labor income as well as nonlabor income from substantial wealth.

6.1. Trends in U.S. Wealth Inequality

There are two easily accessible sources of U.S. data on the distribution of wealth and the evolution of wealth inequality over time. The first source is the Distributional Financial Accounts (DFA) data.[1] Researchers at the Board of Governors of the Federal Reserve System use aggregate data on assets and liabilities from the quarterly Financial Accounts of the United States to determine the total net worth of U.S. households. Then, information from the triennial Survey of Consumer Finances, interpolated between survey years, is used to distribute the assets of various types and the liabilities to individual households. DFA estimates of the shares of US wealth owned by those in different percentiles of the wealth distribution are available from the third quarter of 1989 to the present.

The second data source is the annual distributional national accounts presented in the World Inequality Database (WID).[2] These wealth estimates are derived largely by capitalizing the income payments from various assets as declared on income tax returns. The capitalization method uses the arithmetical link between the value of an asset and the income generated by that asset. For example, if I declare $5 in dividend payments on my income tax return and the typical dividend yield is estimated to be 10%, then the value of my wealth held in shares would be estimated as $5/.10 = $50. WID wealth inequality estimates for U.S. individual taxpayers are available for the years from 1962 to 2019. These two measures of the distribution of wealth involve a number of critical assumptions that we cannot address here. The interested reader is encouraged to examine the detailed information on methods and measurements on the footnoted web pages.

Figure 6.1 presents DFA and WID data on US wealth inequality over the years available in each data source. While the DFA data are published for each quarter of the year, we use the annual average of these quarterly estimates in order to enhance comparability with the WID estimates. This chart uses a slightly different measure of inequality than we have seen

---

[1] https://www.federalreserve.gov/releases/z1/dataviz/dfa/index.html.
[2] https://wid.world/country/usa/.

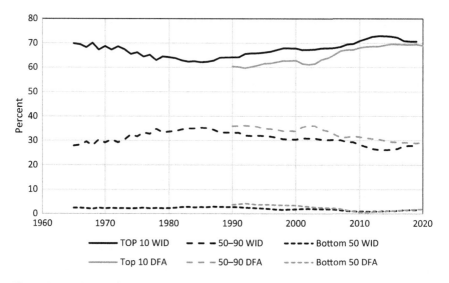

Figure 6.1:   Shares of Wealth Owned by the Top 10%, Middle 50–90% and Bottom 50%

Sources: WID from the World Inequality Database, https://wid.world/country/usa/ and DFA from the Distributed Financial Accounts, https://www.federalreserve.gov/releases/z1/dataviz/dfa/index.html.

thus far. Instead of measuring the wealth levels associated with different percentiles of the distribution, Figure 6.1 plots the shares of total wealth owned by those in the top 10%, the middle 50% to 90% and the bottom 50% of the distribution in each year. Both the DFA approach to allocating total wealth to households on the basis of survey responses and the WID method of capitalizing income from wealth found in individual income tax returns give very similar pictures of the level of wealth inequality in any given year and the trends in wealth inequality over time.

Clearly, total wealth in America is very unequally distributed among individuals and households. For every available year in the two databases, the share of total net worth owned by the richest 10% of the population is far greater than the share owned by all those below the 90th percentile. This is a much greater degree of inequality than we saw in the distribution of U.S. wages.

The WID data indicate that wealth inequality fell during the first two and a half decades charted in Figure 6.1. From 1962 to 1985, the wealth share of the top 10% fell by 8 percentage points, from 70.3% to 62.1%, while the share of those in middle 50th to 90th percentiles increased by

8 points from 27.1% to 35.2%. After 1990, both the WID and DFA data show rising wealth inequality. The WID top 10% wealth share rose to nearly 73% in 2014 before tailing off to 71% in 2019. The DFA top 10% share rose from 60% in 1990 to 70% in 2015 before stabilizing at that level for the rest of the 2010s. Like wage inequality, disparities in the distribution of wealth increased steadily during the last four decades.

Figure 6.1 gives us a clear picture of the extreme nature of U.S. wealth inequality and the steady increase in wealth inequality over time. In order to understand better the magnitude of wealth differences between households at different points of the wealth distribution and how these have changed over time, Table 6.1 presents data for selected years on the average real net worth of households in five percentile groups, measured in 2019 prices. Top 10 refers to the 10% with the highest wealth ownership while 50–75 identifies the 25% with real wealth from the 50th to the 75th percentiles of the distribution. These data are from the triennial Survey of Consumer Finances that is the basis for the Federal Reserve's estimation of the DFA wealth shares discussed above.

The average real wealth of households in the top 10% of the wealth distribution dwarfs that of households in the other percentile groups in every year. In 2019, the average real wealth of the top 10 households, at nearly $6 million, was 8 times the average real wealth of households in the 75–90 percentile group and 24 times that of households in the 50–75 group. Those in the bottom 25% of households had negative net worth of –$15,100 as total debt exceeded the value of their assets. Ownership of 70% of the total American net worth translates into an incredible monetary advantage for the typical top 10 household.

Table 6.1:   Average Real Wealth by Percentile Group, Selected Years

	Top 10	75–90	50–75	25–50	Bottom 25
2019	$5,729,600	$703,600	$236,300	$58,100	–$13,500
2010	$4,378,800	$622,000	$198,900	$42,000	–$15,100
2007	$4,919,900	$725,800	$281,100	$71,700	–$2,800
1998	$3,049,200	$506,600	$202,200	$56,500	–$2,900
1989	$2,470,000	$449,400	$177,000	$45,700	–$1,200

Source: Survey of Consumer Finances, Historical Tables, estimates inflation-adjusted to 2019 dollars at https://www.federalreserve.gov/econres/scfindex.htm.

Consistent with the evidence of increasing U.S. wealth inequality in Figure 6.1, the growth rate of average real net worth from 1989 to 2019 was fastest at higher percentiles of the wealth distribution. The average real wealth of the richest households more than doubled from $2,470,000 in 1989 to $5,729,600 in 2019. The households in the 75–90 percentile group saw their average wealth grow at a substantially slower rate of 56% from 1989 to 2019 while the real mean wealth of households in the 50–75 group increased by just a third to $236,300 in 2019. The average real wealth of those in the 25–50 percentiles grew by 28% over the three decades while net worth for those in the lowest percentile group fell from –$1,200 in 1989 to –$13,500 in 2019. The ratio of average real wealth of the top 10 households to that of the households in the 25–50 percentile group rose from 54.0 to 98.6.

The sharp drop in house prices and the stock market during the financial crisis and great recession led to large declines in average real wealth for households at every point of the U.S. wealth distribution. But, while average real wealth declined by 11% from 2007 to 2010 for the top 10, the rates of decrease were 14% for those in the 75–90 percentile group, 29% for those in the 50–75 group and 41% for those in the 25–50 percentile group. The recovery after 2010 did push average real wealth for the top 10 above the 2007 level but for the other percentile groups included in Table 6.1, average real wealth had not regained 2007 values even by 2019. For households in the 75–90 percentile group, the 2019 average real wealth was 97% of the 2007 value while the corresponding figure was 84% for the 50–75 group and 81% for the 25–50 percentile group. The bottom 25 registered negative real wealth of –$13,500 in 2019 well below the 2007 figure of –$2,800. Clearly, the financial crisis and great recession had a pronounced negative effect on average real wealth that were bigger for households in lower percentiles groups and that persisted at least until 2019 for households outside the top 10 at least.

At this point, you might be wondering what policies might be proposed to change the highly unequal distribution of wealth and income among U.S. households. That, along with a discussion of the case for undertaking policy in the first place, is the topic of Chapter 7.

6.2. Drivers of U.S. Wealth Inequality

In his widely read and highly influential book, Thomas Piketty (2014) presents a comprehensive analysis of the history of wealth inequality in

France, England, Germany and the U.S. He identifies four primary drivers of rising wealth inequality since 1980. These are increases in asset prices, especially the prices of shares of stock and houses; the rise of very highly compensated "super managers", especially in U.S. enterprises; the tendency for the rate of return on assets to exceed the rate of growth of total income, leading to a rising ratio of wealth to income; and the role of gifts and inheritance in lengthening the period of compound growth of wealth. Here, we examine each of these in turn.

6.2.1. *Rising Asset Prices*

The 1980s marked a turning point away from the tightly regulated financial services industry of the post-war era and toward a deregulated industry with the rapid development of new methods of financing expenditures and new investment vehicles for accumulating savings. Piketty (2014) argues that financial deregulation triggered a long-run catch-up phenomenon in asset prices, formerly restrained by government regulations, that accelerated in the 1980s and 1990s and continued into the 21st century. These rising asset prices stimulated by deregulation and growth of the economy led to an increase in the value of U.S. assets. Figure 6.2 presents two indicators of the evolution of house prices and the price of shares of stock from 1975 to the present that are readily available in the FRED database maintained by the Federal Reserve Bank of St. Louis.

The share price index exhibits huge increases in the value of U.S. stock shares from 1975 to 2021 with major downward corrections from the dot-com bust of 2001 to 2003 and the financial crisis of 2008 to 2009 and minor decreases in 2016 and 2020. Share prices rose by 1,307.1% from 1975 to 2001, fell by 20% from 2001 to 2003, rose again by 77.2% from 2003 to 2007, fell by 35.1% from 2007 to 2009 and then rose by 159.5% from 2009 to 2021. Over the whole period from 1970 to 2021, the share price index advanced by 3,259.6%. It is important to note that the share price index in Figure 6.2 is a fairly conservative indicator of changes in the average price of U.S. shares since it is based on all shares of stock traded on public exchanges. In comparison, the NASDAQ composite index, which is more heavily weighted toward technology stocks, rose by 12,020.1% from 1975 to 2021.

The price index for all house sales also exhibits substantial gains, rising steadily by 756.7% from 1975 to 2021 with the exception of a fairly long six-year pause following the financial crisis. The index rose

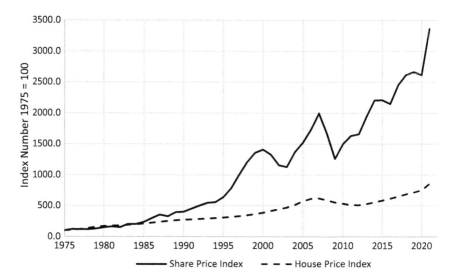

Figure 6.2:   U.S. Housing and Stock Price Indices (1975 = 100)

Source: The Share Price Index is the annual average Total Share Prices for All Shares for the United States developed by the OECD and available at https://fred.stlouisfed.org/series/SPASTT01USM661N. The House Price Index is the annual average All Transactions House Price Index for the United States developed by the U.S. Federal Housing Finance Agency and available at https://fred.stlouisfed.org/series/USSTHPI.

by 519.2% from 1975 to 2007, then fell by 14.5% from 2007 to 2013 before rising again by 61.7 % from 2013 to 2021. The two asset prices identified by Piketty (2014) indeed rose by a considerable amount over the last four and half decades.

Kuhn, Schularick and Steins (2020) examine the implications of these asset price developments, which generate gains in net worth for those owning a house or shares of stock, for the U.S. wealth distribution. Because of differences in wealth portfolios of the rich and middle class, they describe the distributional effects as a "race" between the housing and stock market. Since households in the 50th to 90th percentiles of the wealth distribution have a higher proportion of their wealth in their owner-occupied houses, an increase in house prices would increase their share of total wealth leading to less wealth inequality. On the other hand, households in the top 10% of the wealth distribution have a higher proportion of their wealth in shares of stock so that a rise in stock prices would add to their share of total wealth and result in greater wealth inequality.

Kuhn, Shularick and Steins (2020) estimate the effect of this race between housing and stock markets on the share of wealth held by the richest 10% of households. From 1971 to 2016, this share increased by 8.2 percentage points but in the counterfactual case of no increase in stock prices, the top 10% share of total wealth would have increased by just 4.9 percentage points. These estimates exhibit a large impact of the change in stock prices from 1971 to 2016 on the share of wealth held by the top 10%. An alternative estimate indicates that in the counterfactual case of no increase in house prices, the share of wealth held by the top 10% would have increased by 10.4 percentage points. This is because there would have been no house price boost to the wealth share of households below the 90th percentile of the wealth distribution. From Figure 6.2, we can easily see that the stock market won the race with the house market by a large margin after 1975 and the differential gains in asset values from these changes help explain the rise in wealth inequality depicted in Figure 6.1 over the same period.

6.2.2. *Compensation of Super Managers*

While current wealth inequality in the U.S. is nearing the 1910 heights of the Gilded Age, when the richest 10% of households owned 80% of total assets, one major difference between these two eras has been emphasized by Piketty (2014). In the Gilded Age, the richest American households received the vast majority of their income from profits, dividends and rents generated by their ownership of business enterprises and agricultural land. However, today most of the income of the richest households consists of wages and salaries and other compensation from employment, a phenomenon that Piketty dubs the rise of super managers.

This is relevant to our discussion of wealth inequality trends because, as we have seen in previous chapters, the wages and salaries of the highest-paid employees increased dramatically after 1980. Bakija, Cole and Heim (2012) painstakingly examine the occupations pursued by individuals in the top 1% of employees as revealed by income tax returns. Executives and managers of businesses outside of the financial services industry, like those in manufacturing or trade, plus financial professionals accounted for 43.7% of top earners in 1979 and 44.9% in 2005. By way of contrast, doctors and lawyers were 23.8% of top earners in 1979 and 24.1% in 2005. More importantly, business executives and financial professionals among the top 1% of U.S. taxpayers increased their share of national income from 5.4% in 1979 to 9.1% in 2005, accounting for fully 60% of the increased share of national income going to the top 1% of taxpayers between those years.

Others document the sharp rise in top business salaries over the past few decades. For example, Bebchuck and Grinstein (2005) find that the average compensation of the five highest-paid executives at S&P 500 corporations, adjusted for inflation, more than doubled in just ten years, from $9.5 million in 1993 to $21.4 million in 2003. Kaplan and Rauh (2013) estimate that the average, inflation-adjusted, pay of the 25 highest-paid hedge fund managers rose from $133.7 million in 2002 to $537.2 million in 2012. And Mishel and Kandra (2021) report that CEO compensation rose 1,322% from 1978 to 2020.

Since higher-income individuals tend to save a higher fraction of their income and use these savings to acquire financial and nonfinancial assets, this rapid increase in income earned by those in high-level business positions would have increased both wage and wealth inequality. In addition to high and growing incomes leading to increased wealth accumulation through savings, a significant share of top business executive compensation comes in the form of equity in the firm. Bebchuck and Grinstein (2005) find that the share of equity in the compensation of the five highest-paid executives in the S&P 500 firms rose from 37% in 1993 to 55% in 2003. In addition, Mishel and Kandra (2021) report that vested stock awards amounted to 83.1% of average CEO compensation in 2020. Obviously, this type of compensation structure adds directly to the net worth of highly paid business executives and finance professionals.

Much has been written about the causes of sharply rising executive pay. Kaplan and Rauh (2013) provide a review of the main theories and available evidence. Piketty's reference to "super" managers reflects one leading explanation that goes back to Sherwin Rosen's (1981) classic paper on the economics of superstars. This would trace increased managerial compensation to increased managerial productivity arising from the growth in markets triggered by new information and communications technology, the expansion of international trade, and new opportunities to organize the production process across international borders. In addition, tournament theory suggests that high executive salaries are necessary to provide incentives for lower-tier employees to undertake the effort and skill acquisition necessary to compete for top positions when they become vacant. Finally, some see high CEO salaries as resulting from their strong bargaining position, stemming from the makeup and practices of the compensation committees of corporate boards. All of these factors likely combine to provide an explanation for the high and rising salaries of star managers.

6.2.3. *Return on Assets Relative to Income Growth* ($r > g$)

The arithmetical inequality $r > g$ is the centerpiece of Piketty's (2014) analysis of long-run trends in the ratio of wealth to income and has been the focus of much of the academic response to his theory (Mankiw 2015). In this relationship, r stands for the real, or inflation-adjusted, rate of return on financial and nonfinancial assets and equals the sum of profits, rents, dividends, interest, royalties and capital gains (nonlabor income) received by households as a percentage of their total real wealth. And g represents the growth rate of the total real labor and nonlabor income created by economic activity during a given time period. If over some period of time $r > g$, then nonlabor income will increase as a fraction of total income. If those receiving nonlabor income tend to save most of it and use these savings to buy additional assets, then total wealth will increase relative to annual income. Finally, if the distribution of wealth is unequal at the beginning of this time period, then this process generating faster growth in nonlabor income and asset accumulation would lead to greater wealth and total income inequality.

Piketty doesn't provide a theoretical rationale for why r might be greater than g but, rather, claims this has been an historical tendency for most high-income economies. He estimates that in recent decades, r has been 4–5% and income growth has been slower than that because of declining population and productivity growth. For example, U.S. real gross national income increased at an average annual rate of 2.7% over the years from 1980 to 2019 as compared with 3.8% from 1948 to 1979. On the basis of this historical tendency for $r > g$, Piketty forecasts continued increases in wealth inequality as the 21st century unfolds.

In addition to the average return on wealth exceeding income growth as a factor leading to greater wealth inequality, some very recent research provides evidence for considerable heterogeneity in the returns to wealth, with richer households and individuals enjoying greater than average real rates of return on their financial and nonfinancial assets. This gives greater scope to the argument that saving out of nonlabor income amplifies inequality in the distribution of wealth. Because Norway imposes a direct tax on wealth, economists have access to very detailed data on the assets and income sources of Norwegian taxpayers. Fagereng *et al.* (2020) take advantage of these data to study the rate of return to wealth over the period 2004–2015 for 33 million Norwegians. They find that the annual real rate of return to total net worth averaged 11% for those at the 90th percentile of the wealth distribution, 3.2% for those at the 50th percentile and –3.1% (debts exceeded the value of assets) for those at the 10th percentile. At the 90th percentile, the average rate of return on equity in private business and on risky financial assets was as high as 30–35%, well above the returns on similar assets for taxpayers at lower percentiles of the Norwegian wealth distribution.

Inês Xavier (2021) attempts a similar analysis for U.S. households using data from the Survey of Consumer Finances for 1989–2019. This survey information is more limited and for much smaller samples than the Norwegian tax data. In addition, the survey is carried out only every three years which complicates the estimation of annual real rates of return. However, like the results for Norway, Xavier (2021) finds strong evidence of a positive correlation between the average real rate of return and the level of wealth across households. For households in the 20th–90th percentiles of the wealth distribution, the average real rate of return varied between 3.3% and 3.9% while for those above the 90th percentile, the corresponding range was 3.1% to 8.3%. In both studies, the rate of return difference appears to reflect personal characteristics, such as education, that could affect an individual's ability to make particularly good decisions about asset purchases out of savings. However, fixed costs of investing, such as minimum purchase requirements and the time and effort expended in evaluating alternative assets, are also important in giving an edge to those who have greater amounts to invest.

6.2.4. *Inheritance and Gifts*

Piketty (2014) identifies inheritance as an important factor leading to the amplification of wealth inequality in the Gilded Age and a factor that has again become important in recent years. However, it is difficult to obtain accurate data on the amount of wealth inherited or given during a period of time. There are three methods available to researchers. In some countries, like France and Sweden, comprehensive inheritance and gift tax programs generate very detailed data for individuals. In the U.S., however, inheritance taxes are applied only to very large estates and so there is limited information from this source. A second method is to use the responses to surveys, like the Survey of Consumer Finances, to identify the relative importance of inheritance and gifts as a source of wealth for individuals. Problems with this type of source stem from the fairly small samples covered and measurement error from the limited knowledge about household wealth of some survey respondents. Finally, an aggregate estimate of inheritance can be derived from the profile of wealth by age, using age-specific mortality rates to predict deaths.

A long-run perspective on the relative importance of inheritance and gifts in total wealth is provided by Alvaredo, Garbinti and Piketty (2017). This is also an excellent source of information on the various methods and assumptions used in estimating intergenerational wealth transfers. For the U.S., they estimate that such transfers as a percentage of total wealth peaked at 65% in 1930 and fell to approximately 50% in the two decades from 1970 to 1990. After 1990, the share of total U.S. wealth accounted for by inheritance and gifts rose to nearly 65%, depending on the method used to estimate gifts. Their estimates of the inheritance and gift share of total wealth for France, Germany, Great Britain and Sweden vary from 50% to 60% in 2010. By this account, intergenerational transfers account for a substantial amount of the value of assets owned by individuals and households in these countries.

Feiveson and Sabelhaus (2018) use the Survey of Consumer Finances to demonstrate that inheritance and gifts play an important role in increasing wealth inequality. We can summarize three empirical conclusions from their study:

1. The majority of intergenerational wealth transfers go to already rich households. Over the years from 1995 to 2016, 56% of the value of wealth transfers went to households in the top 10% of the wealth distribution while just 8% of the value of inheritance and gifts went to those in the bottom 50% of the wealth distribution.
2. However, inheritance and gifts are a more important source of wealth for the poorest households because they own relatively few financial and nonfinancial assets. In 2016, households in the bottom half of the wealth distribution, who owned 3% of total wealth, had 74% of their wealth from inheritance and gifts. In contrast, the wealthiest 10% of households, who owned 73% of total wealth, had 53% of their wealth from inheritance and gifts.

3. The distribution of inheritance and gifts adds to overall wealth inequality. The richest 10% of households owned 73% of the total value of financial and nonfinancial assets in 2016. However, if all inheritance and gifts received during the years from 1995 to 2016 were distributed equally among all households, the share of the richest 10% would be just 40%.

As argued by Piketty (2014) stock and housing prices, the level and composition of executive compensation, the tendency for $r > g$ at least in the short run and the importance of intergenerational wealth transfers all changed over the years since 1980 in a way that would increase the degree of inequality in the distribution of wealth in America.

6.3. Racial Wealth Gaps

Recall that our examination of racial and gender wage differentials in Chapter 2 suggested that these contributed relatively little to the evolution of U.S. wage inequality after 1980. Since racial disparities in wealth far exceed those stemming from wage differentials, it is important to consider the potential contribution of racial wealth gaps to the rise in U.S. wealth inequality portrayed in Figure 6.1 and Table 6.1. While much has been written on this topic, we focus on a very recent study of long-run trends in the wealth of black and white, more accurately nonblack, U.S. residents.

Ellora Derenoncourt and colleagues (2022) use Census data, state tax reports, various nongovernmental sources and the Survey of Consumer Finances to compile a times series of data on the average wealth of African-Americans and Americans of other races for 1860–2022. They find evidence of considerable wealth convergence in the first four decades following emancipation. The nonblack to black wealth ratio fell from 60 to 1 in 1860 to 10 to 1 by 1920 and then to 7 to 1 by 1970. African-Americans accumulated valuable assets during this period at a faster pace than whites and other racial groups despite Jim Crow laws enforced by lynchings and the expropriation of property in the south and the federal government's support for strict segregation in urban real estate markets in the north. The relative prosperity of Tulsa's "Black Wall Street" and its destruction during the 1922 race riots illustrate the rewards of wealth accumulation to the black community and the catastrophic risks to their wealth during the Jim Crow era.

Their time series data also shows that convergence stopped after 1970 and the nonblack to black average wealth ratio remained around the 7 to 1 level until 2020 despite the passage of civil rights legislation and the end of legal forms of discrimination. Black wealth accumulation was slowed by relatively low levels of initial average wealth among black households, by relatively slower black income and savings growth after 1980 and by the tendency for black asset portfolios to be less heavily weighted by shares of stock and other financial assets that, as we have seen, generated substantial capital gains. Note that, according to the 2019 Survey of Consumer Finances, 46.6% of black households had savings in comparison to 62.8% of white households and 4.7% of black households owned stock assets in comparison to 17.5% of white households.

Figure 6.3 provides perspective on the evolution of the average wealth of different racial groups since 1989. The Survey of Consumer Finances reports the average real net worth (assets minus liabilities in 2019 prices) for households that identify themselves as white non-Hispanic, black non-Hispanic and Hispanic. A fourth category includes households that are of any other race or mixed-race group. These estimates are plotted in

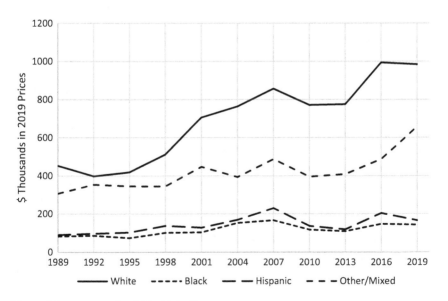

Figure 6.3:   Average Real Wealth by Race

Source: Survey of Consumer Finances, Historical Tables, Estimates inflation-adjusted to 2019 dollars at https://www.federalreserve.gov/econres/scfindex.htm.

Figure 6.3 and demonstrate a huge difference in average wealth between white, black and Hispanic households. In 1989, white households had net worth equal to $452,000, or $370,000 more than the average wealth of black and Hispanic households. From 1989 to 2019, the average real net worth of white households more than doubled increasing by 117% while the growth rate of average real net worth for black (Hispanic) households was 73% (84%). As a result, the racial wealth gap between white and black and Hispanic households increased over the three decades in the graph. From 1989 to 2019, the white-black wealth ratio grew from 5.5 to 6.9 while the white-Hispanic ratio went from 5.0 to 5.9.

The average real wealth of households in the other/mixed race category, which includes Asian-Americans, is much closer to the white household levels and increased rapidly in the years following the financial crisis and great recession. Still, the average wealth of white households was one and a half times that of the other/mixed race households in both 1989 and 2019. While these trends clearly reflect differences between groups in the extent to which they benefited from the bull market in shares, rising house prices, the opportunities for high executive pay and the initial levels of wealth across groups, they give us another perspective on the increased wealth inequality experienced in America since the 1970s.

6.4. Income Inequality

We now turn to an examination of changes over time in the distribution of total income among U.S. households. Once again, total household income includes the labor earnings of individual household members and the non-labor income generated by the ownership of financial and nonfinancial assets. Given our analysis of changes over time in wage inequality and disparities in the ownership of assets, it would be very surprising to find that household income inequality did not increase over the decades since 1980. This is particularly true given that the likelihood of marriage between individuals with similar levels of education and other personal characteristics that have been found to be determinants of wage potential has increased significantly over time (Greenwood *et al.* 2014). Also relevant is the positive link between wealth and high labor income discussed above. Given rising inequality in the labor and nonlabor sources of household income, an important question concerns the impact of social insurance, taxes and government transfer payments on the inequality of spendable household income.

The Congressional Budget Office (CBO) prepares an annual report analyzing the distribution of total U.S. household income and the effect of social insurance income, transfer payments and federal taxes on income inequality. Their report[3] for 2021 provides comprehensive information on income inequality in 2018 and trends from 1979 to 2018, drawn from income tax and survey data.

We start with the CBO's estimates of changes over time in the distribution of household market income, which is defined as the compensation of workers plus the income accruing to owners of financial and real assets. In addition to wage and salary payments and income from wealth including capital gains, this income measure includes employer contributions to health insurance and employer payroll taxes. Figure 6.4 plots the average market income, measured in 2018 prices, received by households in each quintile of the household income distribution. Each quintile includes one-fifth of the total number of households, so top 20 refers to the 20% with the highest incomes while 40–60 identifies the 20% with incomes from the 40th to the 60th percentiles of the distribution.

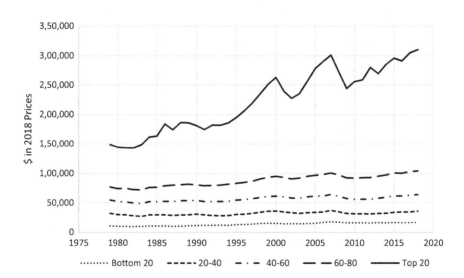

Figure 6.4:   Average Household Market Income by Quintile, 1979–2018

Source: https://www.cbo.gov/publication/57061. Income is in terms of 2018 prices and includes labor income and income from wealth. See text for definitions.

---

[3] Available at https://www.cbo.gov/publication/57061.

Figure 6.4 illustrates rising household income inequality over time as the average real income of households in the highest quintile increased at a much faster pace than the average income of those in the lower four income quintiles. Average income, in 2018 prices, of households in the top quintile more than doubled from $148,700 in 1979 to $310,000 in 2018. This reflects the rapid rise in the wages earned by high-wage workers, the growing concentration of wealth in the hands of the wealthiest and the increasing share of income going to wealth owners that we have discussed above. Note that average real market income for this group has two peaks in 2000 and 2007 which were both followed by sharp decreases. This reflects the high fraction of income from the direct and indirect ownership, via investment funds and retirement accounts, of stock for this group of households and the impact of the dot-com stock market bubble and the financial crisis on the value and income from this form of wealth.

As we saw with labor income, income inequality increased the fastest at the very top of the distribution of market income. I did not plot the average market income of households in the top 1% of the distribution because doing so would distort the graph and make it difficult to distinguish among the lower quintiles. The CBO estimate of the average real market income of the top 1% of households more than tripled from $579,100 in 1979 to $1,987,500 in 2018.

Increased inequality is also indicated by the diverging growth paths in average income among households in the middle three quintiles, even though income growth for these groups was quite modest from 1979 to 2018 and the growing gaps between them are not easy to see in the chart. Average income for the 60–80 group rose by 36% while the rate of increase was 17% for the 40–60 quintile and 12% in the 20–40 category. Average inflation-adjusted income for the lowest quintile rose by 60%, which significantly narrowed the gap with average income in the middle of the distribution, but this was from just $10,400 in 1979 to $16,600 in 2018.

6.4.1. *Social Insurance, Transfers and Taxes*

The CBO data allow us to look beyond labor and nonlabor earnings to study trends in the distribution of household income that include income receipts not connected to the current production of goods and services. Figure 6.5 presents estimates of Gini coefficients that describe inequality in three different measures of household income. Recall that the Gini

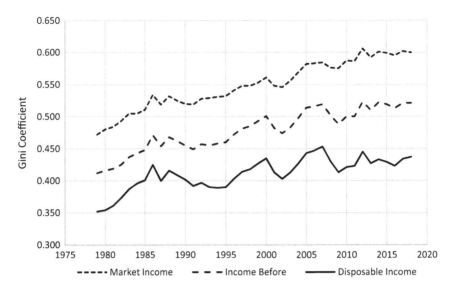

Figure 6.5: Gini Coefficients of Household Income by Income Source, 1979–2018

Source: https://www.cbo.gov/publication/56575. Income Before does not include Federal government transfer payments and taxes. These are included in Disposable Income. See text for details.

coefficient is a measure of the overall degree of inequality in a distribution, taking into account information from all percentiles, that ranges from zero to one with higher values indicating greater inequality. The first measure of household income is market income, which we discussed above.

The second household income measure, income before taxes and transfers, adds receipts from social insurance programs administered by government agencies to the labor and nonlabor income earned by household members. Social insurance income includes Social Security retirement and disability benefits, the value of Medicare health insurance, Unemployment Insurance payments to eligible out-of-work individuals and Worker's Compensation insurance benefits to covered workers who were injured on the job.

Finally, disposable income adds household receipts of means-tested government transfer payments to income before taxes and transfers and then deducts federal tax payments. Of the three income measures, this is the most comprehensive accounting of cash resources available to households. Means-tested transfer payments include a number of cash benefits from federal and state government programs designed to supplement the income of qualified low-income households. The two most important, accounting for 70% of total transfers, are health insurance benefits from Medicaid and the Children's Health Insurance Program or CHIP. Federal tax payments include income, payroll and excise taxes paid by the household and corporate income taxes allocated to shareholders. No adjustment is made for state and local taxes.

Figure 6.5 supports two conclusions about the distribution of U.S. household income over time. The first is that adding social insurance benefits to market income and adjusting for taxes and transfer payments clearly lowers income inequality as measured by Gini coefficients. On average, the Gini coefficient for market incomes is 15% higher than the Gini coefficient for income before taxes and transfers and 33% greater than the Gini for disposable income. Social insurance income and transfer payments are relatively more important for lower-income households and the effective federal tax rates are progressively higher for higher-income households. Households in the lowest three quintiles, those at or below the 60th percentile, earned 22.4% of market income, 25.9% of income before taxes and transfers and 32.9% of disposable income. Federal government programs to redistribute income to lower-income households significantly lower measured inequality.

Second, despite the redistributive effects of social insurance and the tax and transfer system on the level of inequality in any given year, these programs did not have a significant effect on the trend in household income inequality. The three lines in Figure 6.5 generally follow parallel tracks from 1979 to 2018. The Gini coefficient for market income increased by 27%, from .472 to .600 from 1979 to 2018. The Gini coefficient for income before taxes and transfers increased by 26% and the Gini for disposable income rose by 24% over the same time period. Increasing wage inequality, increasing concentration in the ownership of wealth and increasing inequality in nonlabor income all contributed to a substantial rise in household income inequality even after taking into account social insurance receipts, transfer income and federal tax payments.

Figure 6.6 illustrates the effect of social insurance payments, taxes and transfers on inequality at the extremes of the household income distribution by comparing the shares of income before and after social insurance, taxes and transfers received by the top 1% and bottom 20% of households. The income share of the top 1% is substantially reduced when

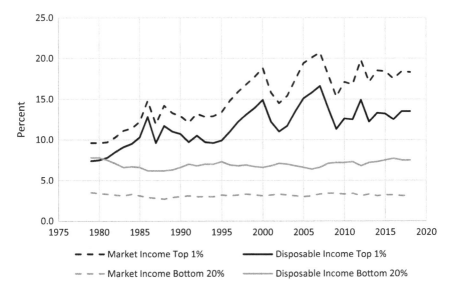

Figure 6.6: Income Shares of the Top 1% and Bottom 20% of Households
Source: See note to Figure 6.6.

income is defined to include receipts from federal government programs and exclude tax payments while the income share of the bottom 20% of households increases considerably. In 2018, top 1% households received 18% of total market income but 13.5% of income after taxes and transfers while 3.2% of market income went to households in the bottom 20% of the income distribution versus 7% of income after taxes and transfers. The solid black and gray lines in Figure 6.6 are considerably closer together than the dashed lines.

The income share of the top 1% of households clearly shows the effect of the substantial decreases in the stock market starting in 2001 and 2007. Despite these sharp downturns, the share of disposable income going to the richest households almost doubled from 7.4% in 1979 to 13.5% in 2018. Interestingly, the bottom 20% share of both market income and income including social insurance, transfers and taxes is roughly constant over the four decades depicted in the chart. The increased income share of households in the top 1% came largely at the expense of middle- and lower-middle-income households. The share of disposable income for those in the 20th to 40th percentiles fell from 12.3% in 1979 to 10.7% in 2018 and the income share of households in the 40th–60th percentiles dropped from 16.4% in 1979 to 14.4% in 2018.

6.4.2. *Income Inequality During the Pandemic*

Thus far, we have been examining long-run trends in wage, wealth and income inequality. In so doing, I have often chosen to focus on data ending in 2019 even when information for later years is available. This is because of the unique aspects of post-2019 economic developments that largely resulted from government policies around the world to control the spread of the COVID-19 virus. A number of inequality issues, such as disparities in the incidence of serious illness, in the risk of unemployment and in the ability to work from home, have been raised in media coverage of the pandemic. So, we now turn to a review of short-run changes in income inequality over the period from March 2020, when the pandemic began to be felt in full force, to the present.

We are able to do so because of recent efforts to develop monthly measures of income inequality. Blanchet, Saez and Zucman (2020) describe the process of combining publicly available data from an array of different sources to estimate the "real-time" monthly distribution of income before and after taxes, transfer payments and retirement income.[4]

One of the unique aspects of the pandemic recession was the very rapid rise in unemployment from 4.4% of the labor force in March 2020 to 14.7% in April of that year. This was the highest monthly U.S. unemployment rate since the Great Depression. An example of the severity of the unemployment situation is given by Bell *et al.* (2022) who report that, in the year following March 2020, nearly a third of California workers applied for unemployment insurance and half of those receiving benefits did so for six months or more.

The extent of the pandemic recession can be seen in Figure 6.7 which plots changes in the average real market income of households in the top 10%, the 50th–90th percentiles and the bottom 50% of the income distribution from January 2020 to June 2022. In order to emphasize short-run changes, the data are presented as index numbers showing monthly real income relative to the level in January 2020. While all three groups have index numbers set to 100 in January 2020, it is important to note that the

---

[4]These data are available at www.realtimeinequality.org.

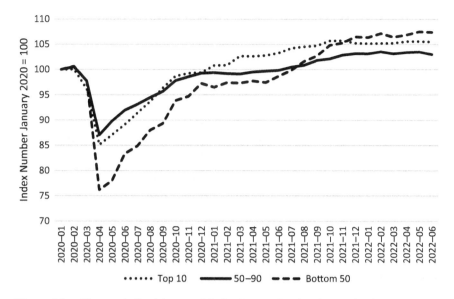

Figure 6.7:   Changes in Real Average Market Income During the Pandemic

Source: Data on real market income per household are from the real-time inequality database at www.
realtimeinequality.org. Values are converted to index numbers by dividing each month's value by that
for January 2020 and multiplying by 100.

real average market income from labor and nonlabor sources was
$587,277 for the top 10%, $116,531 for the middle 40% and just $19,774
for the bottom 50% in that month.

Real market income for all three groups began to fall in February
2020 and plummeted from March to April. The decrease was 24% for
those in the bottom 50%, 13% for those in the 50th–90th percentiles and
15% for the top 10% of households. Labor income fell as a result of bur-
geoning unemployment for workers in all three income groups and, for
mostly higher income groups, nonlabor income decreased as stock prices
fell and business profits declined for many firms, especially those affected
by shutdown policies and consumer fears about contracting the virus
(Chetty *et al.* 2020).

The pandemic recession was also unique in the speed and magnitude
of the monetary and fiscal policy responses taken in response. In order to
keep interest rates low to spur spending and to boost liquidity to prevent
a financial market meltdown, the Federal Reserve created money by buying financial assets at an unprecedented pace. The Fed's asset holdings

grew by \$2.7 trillion from March to July 2020. In addition, Congress passed the \$2.2 trillion Coronavirus Aid, Relief and Economic Security (CARES) Act in March 2020 and followed up with an additional \$910 billion in December of that year. A further fiscal stimulus was provided by the \$1.9 trillion American Rescue Plan passed by Congress and signed by President Biden in March 2021.

As a result of these policy actions, the downturn in the economy was brief. In Figure 6.7, we see that real average market income for all three income groups began to rise in May 2020 and continued to increase until June 2022. After falling fastest in the recession, the average real income of households in the bottom half of the distribution rose the fastest in the recovery, growing by 41% from April 2020 to June 2022. The rate of increase over the same period was 24% for households in the top 10% and 18% for those in the middle 40%. However, when measured over the entire period from the beginning of 2020, income growth was much more modest. The distribution of market income widened slightly over the pandemic years with households in the top 10% increasing their share of income from 51% in January 2020 to 51.4% in June 2022. The bottom 50% also increased their share from 8.6% to 8.8% over that time span.

The fiscal stimulus programs passed by Congress consisted of direct checks sent to households, expansion in the coverage and benefits provided by the unemployment insurance program and forgivable loans to prop up small businesses and protect the jobs of their employees via the Paycheck Protection Program. Figure 6.8 helps us see the effect of these programs on average real disposable household income, which includes income from social insurance programs and government transfer payments and subtracts tax payments. Again, this graph plots index numbers to emphasize changes over the pandemic years.

There is no sign in Figure 6.8 of the early 2020 marked decrease in real average income that we see in Figure 6.7. This is because of the automatic stabilizers built into the tax and transfer program. A decrease in market income also decreases tax liabilities and makes households newly eligible for unemployment insurance benefits, nutrition assistance and other transfer payments. As a result, disposable income is somewhat insulated from the impact of business downturns.

Figure 6.8 clearly shows the impact of the three federal stimulus packages on the real average disposable income of the two lowest income groups, with sharp but temporary jumps in the month after each program was enacted. The real average disposable income of households in the

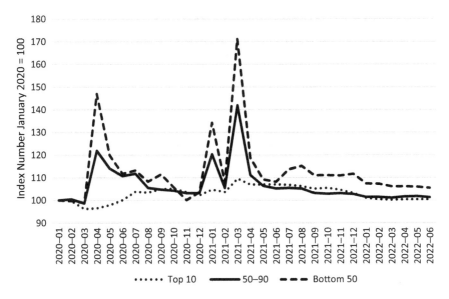

Figure 6.8:   Changes in Real Average Disposable Income During the Pandemic

Source: See footnote to Figure 6.7.

bottom 50% of the income distribution was 70% higher in March 2021 than it was in January 2020. While temporary, these infusions of cash to low-income households allowed them to pay off debt and increase savings. Autor *et al.* (2022) estimate that two-thirds of the PPP payouts went to business owners or their suppliers and creditors and that unemployment insurance enhancements also aided higher-income households by making the self-employed eligible for benefits. However, there is no evidence from the real-time inequality estimates in Figure 6.8 of a major effect of the stimulus programs on the disposable income of top 10% households. The slowing of income growth for all three groups in the first half of 2022 likely reflects the expiration of expanded child tax and earned income tax credits (Blanchet, Saez and Zucman 2022).

For the entire period from January 2020 to June 2022, average real household disposable income grew by 0.4% for the top 10%, 1.3% for households in the 50th–90th percentiles and 5.5% for the bottom 50%. This suggests a reduction in real disposable income inequality among households over the pandemic period. Indeed, the share of income going to the top 10% of households fell slightly, from 45.1% in January 2020 to

44.6% in June 2022, while the income share of households in the bottom 50% increased a bit, from 13.7% to 14.2%. This is not much of a dent in what was an extremely unequal distribution to begin with and concerns remain about the long-run effects from disparities in the incidence of COVID-19 (Tan, Hinman and Abdel 2021), differences in the impact of remote learning on elementary school students (Mervosh 2022) and the drop in enrollments at Community Colleges and regional public universities after 2019 (Anderson and Douglas-Gabriel 2021). On the other hand, some optimism about declining inequality has been taken from the wage increases stemming from the emergence of very tight labor markets in 2022 and a new interest in unionization among service sector employees.

6.5. Summary

Inequality in the distribution of total spendable income among households, including those with just one member, reflects inequality in labor earnings amplified by inequality in the income received from the ownership of real and financial assets less payments on debt. In addition, government programs of social insurance, redistribution through transfer payments and taxation have significant effects on the standard of living of many households. Our purpose in this chapter has been to examine trends in the U.S. distribution of wealth and household income.

The distribution of household wealth is very unequal. Whether wealth is measured by survey responses or capitalizing income reported on tax returns, the current share of total wealth owned by households at or above the 90th percentile of the wealth distribution is about 70%. Wealth inequality has also increased over time. In 1980, the share of the top 10% of households was 65%. Important drivers of this increase have been stock prices rising much faster than house prices; rapid growth in the wages and salaries paid to top earners and the enhanced use of stock grants to compensate business executives; the tendency for the returns on wealth, especially for high-net-worth households, to grow faster than the overall growth of total income; and the intergenerational transfer of wealth by gifts and inheritance. Racial wealth gaps have also widened over the last three decades.

With U.S. wage and wealth inequality growing over time, it is inevitable to see that inequality in total household labor and nonlabor, or market, income has also increased significantly over time. But, due to federal government redistributive programs, inequality of disposable household income is much lower than market income inequality. Social insurance payments and transfers raise the disposable income of those at the bottom of the distribution while the slightly progressive nature of federal taxes lowers the disposable income of rich households more than for those with lower income levels. However, the trend toward increased U.S. income inequality over time is also true for disposable income. While it is perhaps too early for an assessment of the COVID-19 pandemic on inequality, recent data show the powerful effect of the automatic stabilizers in the tax and transfer system in insulating disposable income from recession. The massive federal stimulus programs enacted in 2020 and the beginning of 2021 had a very important, albeit temporary, impact on disposable income for middle- and low-income households.

Chapter 7

Consequences and Cures

The conclusion from the evidence we have examined in the previous chapters is that the lion's share of the income and wealth created by U.S. economic growth over the past four decades has accrued to the highest wage earners, the wealthiest individuals and the richest households. As a result, the U.S. stands out among high-income economies as having the greatest degree of inequality, however that is measured. Is this a serious societal problem that should be addressed by public policy? Or is this just the price we have to pay for the benefits of new technology and greater global efficiency and the fair result of an economy that rewards the most productive people? In this closing chapter, we examine the economic, political and social consequences of the seemingly inexorable rise in U.S. inequality that form the foundations of the argument in favor of policy interventions to reduce inequality or, at least, slow its growth. We follow that with a summary of some of the many policy proposals that have been offered in the economics literature, taking into account as best we can the likelihood of their implementation in the polarized U.S. political environment.

One thing that seems clear is that we cannot count on long-run economic forces to return U.S. inequality to a "normal" or "equilibrium" level. Economics often emphasizes the idea that short-run outcomes, say the high profitability of firms in a sector of the economy, provide incentives for agents to make decisions, such as entering high-profit industries with new products, that have the effect of changing outcomes in the long run. In this example, the long-run entry of new firms attracted by high profits will adjust the number of suppliers and the level of product prices so that the profits of firms are just high enough to ensure that the product will be produced. The economist's notion of the long run is not linked to the calendar so it is conceivable that the changes in inequality over the past four decades or so have set into motion forces that will ultimately stop or reverse the trend to greater inequality. However, recent research on the evolution of inequality over long periods casts doubt on this possibility.

Guido Alfani (2021) summarizes the available research on wealth and income inequality in pre-industrial Europe going back to 1300. With the exception of falling wealth inequality during the century following the Black Death, the results of this research effort clearly support the conclusion that inequality increased steadily throughout Europe from 1450 to 1800. Comparing the results from these studies of pre-industrial Europe with the well-documented developments in inequality during the 19th and 20th centuries leads Alfani to conclude that the only period of falling inequality over the centuries following the Black Death was during the "great leveling" from 1910 to 1970. This one episode of declining inequality in European history was largely due to public policy, such as progressive taxation, support for worker rights, anti-monopoly regulations and income redistribution policies.

Peter Lindert and Jeffery Williamson (2016) reach a similar conclusion in their masterful study of U.S. income inequality from 1740 to the present that takes advantage of newly available data on wages, wealth and income in the colonial and pre-industrial eras. They find evidence for two periods of falling U.S. inequality: a brief period from 1774 to 1800 after the revolutionary war and what they call the "greatest" leveling from 1910 to 1970. In contrast, the growth and development of the U.S. economy over the long sweep of its history are marked by a steady increase in income inequality with no evidence of incentives for or behavior toward establishing a long-run equilibrium.

Branko Milanovic (2016) concludes that the trend toward greater American wage, wealth and income inequality is likely to continue for the foreseeable future because a "perfect storm" of inequality-increasing forces will put upward pressure on wealth and income inequality in the U.S. Rising future U.S. inequality is likely even if its rate of increase is slowed by demographic forces leading to slower increases in global population and labor force (Goodhart and Pradhan 2020). While much has been made of the tight labor markets seen in the U.S., due in part to slowing growth in the labor force, as the COVID-19 pandemic has waned, it is sobering to note that the share of total labor and nonlabor income going to the top 10% of individuals over 20 increased from 46.6% in August 2019 to 47.2% in August 2022.[1] If we agree that the inequality situation in the U.S. has had major adverse consequences and should be reduced, it appears that public policy will have to take the primary role in bringing that about as opposed to relying on general market forces.

Analysts have identified a number of potentially adverse consequences for individuals, their communities and the nation as a whole from the steady four-decade rise in U.S. inequality. In considering these consequences, it is important to note whether they stem from the economic changes driving increased inequality or from the rise in inequality itself. This is particularly true in considering policy responses.

7.1. Consequences for Individuals

The rise in inequality has certainly had an adverse effect on the wages, wealth and income of the majority of individuals and their families who find themselves at or below the median of the relevant distribution. It's tempting to say that the unequal sharing of the proceeds from economic growth is itself unfair and should be the focus of public policy for that reason alone. However, as we have noted, the question of "fair" and "unfair" is complicated. If the top 10% of workers received the lion's share of increased wages because they made the lion's share of the contribution to economic growth, then many would agree that the labor market outcomes we have studied in this book are fair and should not be altered. Similarly, if people with equal ability have an equal opportunity to gain the education level and skills associated with the biggest increases in wages and income, then the premium to those who chose to pursue higher education levels might be regarded as fair by many. Here, we focus on a few aspects of the impact of rising inequality for individuals that might be more readily described as unfair or that have such substantial consequences for society that policy action is called for.

---

[1] See www.realtimeinequality.org.

7.1.1. *Displaced Workers*

Recall that an important contributing factor to rising inequality has been the hollowing out of the job structure in response to new competition from innovative products, increased imports, technologically driven automation and international outsourcing. This process contributed to rising wage inequality by reducing the fraction of U.S. workers employed in jobs paying wages around the median level. Recall from Table 3.1 that over two million production jobs disappeared in the United States between 2001 and 2019. We don't have the detailed data needed to speak definitively about what happened to the workers who held those jobs but it's a good bet that many had to move to employment in lower-paying occupations, retire earlier than planned or attempt to qualify for disability income. The closest we come is the evidence on the persistent local labor market effects – lower average wages and employment over a decade or more – from exposure to Chinese imports identified by Autor, Dorn and Hanson (2013, 2021). We could say that these workers unfortunately suffered from bad luck. And it's this bad luck that we might argue is an unfair consequence of labor market changes driving increased wage inequality.

Consider that workers make investments in the general skills required to do a job and the particular skills needed to do that job well for a specific employer. Unlike investors in financial assets, workers are largely unable to hedge against risk by diversifying their human capital investments. As a result, job loss from a firm's decision to automate or outsource production has the effect of destroying a portion of the worker's human capital and thus her long-term earnings potential. A large literature supports the conclusions of Kletzer (1998) that displaced workers face long periods of unemployment after losing their jobs and suffer a significant long-term reduction of as much as 20% in their real wage levels once they are reemployed. For example, a recent study of those who lost jobs during the 2008–2009 recession in the state of Washington (Lachowska, Mostad and Setzler 2020) highlights the importance of knowledge and skills that are particularly useful for a given employer. They found that, for those who were displaced from their jobs, earnings when reemployed were roughly 15% less than they would have been with their original employer. This wage disadvantage was seen even for displaced workers hired by firms paying similar average wages as their original employers. This wage penalty associated with the loss of firm-specific human capital was evident even five years after the date of job loss.

Displaced workers appear to pay a high price for being unlucky. A major consequence has been sharply diminished opportunities and labor market prospects for American men without a college degree that have lasting implications for their families and communities (Binder and Bound 2019; Borella, DiNardo and Yang 2019). The risk of ultimate job loss, from globalization or technological change, is very difficult to accurately assess when deciding whether or not to accept a job offer and almost impossible to insure against for the average worker. Public policy might be needed to provide such insurance for workers affected by such inequality increasing shocks to the structure of jobs in the U.S. economy. To be effective, such insurance would have to go beyond the temporary and limited cash assistance provided by the current unemployment insurance system to include longer-term help via training and job search assistance to facilitate their re-employment.

7.1.2. *Health and Risky Behavior*

There is an important adverse effect of both the level of inequality and the economic changes leading to rising inequality in public health. A report on the inequality and health of older Americans by the U.S. Government Accountability Office (2019) uses Health and Retirement Survey data to estimate the proportion of people ages 51–61 in 1992 who were able to live to ages 73–83 in 2014, ranked by their mid-career household earnings. This fraction was 52% for those in the lowest quintile of the earnings distribution, 63% for those in the middle quintile (from the 40th to 60th percentiles) and 74% for those in the highest quintile of the earnings distribution. The report found similar disparities in longevity favoring those in the highest quintiles of the wealth distribution and those with a college degree. This is clear evidence of a significant negative correlation between life expectancy and earnings and wealth inequality, whether or not we regard inequality *per se* as fairly reflecting relative contributions to economic activity.

The research of Anne Case and Angus Deaton (2020) examines the unprecedented three-year decline in life expectancy at birth for the U.S. population from 2014 to 2017. They trace the cause to rapidly rising "deaths of despair" from alcohol abuse, drug overdoses and suicides among white male non-Hispanic Americans ages 45–54 with less than a college degree. In this demographic group, the incidence of deaths from these causes rose from 50 per 100,000 people in 1990 to 160 per 100,000 people in 2017. Over the same period, the death rate stayed fairly constant at 25 per 100,000 people for white, non-Hispanic men with at least a bachelor's degree. While they argue against a direct link between rising inequality and rising rates of deaths of despair, they do point to the consequences of the same labor market changes we have studied in this book as causes of both rising inequality and rising death rates. They cite in particular the long-term loss of jobs paying decent wages to workers with mid-level skills in communities hit by imports, offshoring and technological change. In addition, rising costs and the changing structure of the U.S. healthcare system are also linked to rising deaths of despair.

In *The Broken Ladder*, Keith Payne summarizes considerable experimental evidence from behavioral psychology that establishes a direct link between inequality and the income levels of the lowest earners to behavior that contributes to adverse health and longevity outcomes. There appear to be two main aspects of this relationship. First, those at the lower end of a highly unequal income distribution are more likely to feel needier, make high-risk/high-reward choices and generally engage in riskier behavior. This leads to an increased likelihood of abusing drugs and alcohol that has clear consequences for health and longevity. Second, the importance of relative income comparisons means that inequality is stressful for those at the bottom of the income distribution. This source of increased stress is in addition to the stress associated with the lack of worker control and flexibility and the general demands of most low-pay jobs. In this analysis, the U.S. pattern of rising inequality, with rapid increases in wages, wealth and income at the top and slow-growing or stagnant outcomes for those in the middle of the distribution and below, would be expected to enhance the role of risky behavior and stress in the health situations facing the majority of individuals.

Poor health and increased mortality are not among the things we talk about when economists analyze the short-run losses from imports or technological change. Presumably, the resulting labor market equilibria with lower wages for some and higher wages for others are acceptable to those willing to take the jobs on offer. But there is substantial evidence of serious long-term consequences, such as poor health and increased mortality from risky behavior and stress linked to low wages and inequality, that adversely affects families and communities. This becomes a more serious public health issue when we consider the consequences for workers displaced from their jobs by import competition, offshoring or technological change.

7.1.3. *Intergenerational Effects*

While data linking the labor market outcomes of parents and children are limited, there is fairly substantial evidence of a significant positive inter-generational correlation in the American wage, wealth and income distributions. An acceptance of inequality is based partly on the notions of equal opportunity and pay based on merit so that it is conceivable that a child born to low-income parents can move up the income distribution by accumulating human capital and by working hard. Research showing a significant intergenerational correlation in incomes calls into question the extent of this upward mobility.

Much of the research on intergenerational mobility focuses on estimates of the intergenerational elasticity (IGE) of earnings, income and wealth. For example, Mazumber (2005) uses social security data to estimate the IGE of earnings at 0.60. This means that a father with earnings 10% above average, observed in the period from 1970 to 1985, would be predicted to have children, observed in 1995–1998, with earnings 6% above average. The father's position in the wage distribution is found to have a significant effect on the position of his children in the wage distribution decades later. This is also seen in Lee and Solon (2009) who find a slightly lower but still significant IGE for earnings of 0.44 for sons and 0.43 for daughters. Evidence for declining intergenerational mobility is presented by Davis and Mazumder (2017). They estimate that the American IGE increased from 0.35 for those born between 1942 and 1953 to 0.51 for those in the 1951 to 1964 birth cohort.

In an interesting study, Toney and Robertson (2021) estimate IGEs for the effect of parental and grandparental wealth on the adult income of the third generation. They find that 10% greater parental wealth is associated with 2.5% higher income for the child while 10% greater grandparental wealth is correlated with 2.2% greater income for the grandchild. This might seem like a small effect but recall from Table 6.1 in the last chapter that the average real wealth of households in the top 10% was 2,325% higher than the average real wealth of the median household. Using Toney and Robertson's estimates, this would imply a 580% higher income for children born to parents in the top 10% of the wealth distribution in comparison with children born to parents with the median level of wealth. Taking into account grandparental wealth would enhance this estimated income advantage of children born to top 10% families even further.

Raj Chetty *et al.* (2014, 2017) provide evidence that intergenerational mobility in the U.S. has declined over time. They turn their attention to the percentage of children who earned more than their parents at the same age, comparing those born in 1940 with those born in 1984 by the percentile of parental income. For those whose parents were at the median of the income distribution, 93% of the 1940 cohort had higher adult incomes than their parents while just 50% of the 1984 cohort exceeded their parents' income.

In addition to the direct effect of inheritance, the economic fortunes of children are linked to their parents' income by two factors. Solon (2018) shows that in a steady state equilibrium, the IGE depends on parental investments in the child's human capital, genetic and cultural factors and the interaction of these two. Lower-income parents have fewer resources to devote to the education and health of their children, the decentralized U.S. educational system means that school districts with a high concentration of lower-income families also have fewer resources and the neighborhoods in which many lower-income families live often have a deleterious environmental effect on the health of children growing up there. Given these factors, it is difficult to say that children born to parents at the bottom of the income distribution have opportunities equal to those available to children born to parents at the top of the distribution.

7.2. Consequences for Society

Inequality has also been associated with political and economic issues facing U.S. society. In politics, the rapidly growing income and wealth of the richest households are seen as shifting political power to the rich and contributing to political polarization. In economics, the tendency of high-income families to save more of their income than lower-income families and the tendency of the latter to accumulate high levels of debt is seen as contributing to macroeconomic instability.

7.2.1. *Political Consequences*

Money has always been important to U.S. politics. Supreme Court decisions invalidating legal restrictions on political donations as an infringement on the free speech rights of individuals (*Buckley versus Valeo* 1976) and corporations (*Citizens United versus Federal Election Commission* 2010) have expanded the role of money in elections. At the same time, the rapid rise in the average wealth of the richest households has resulted in a pool of wealthy individuals with substantial means to influence political outcomes. A report by Taylor Giorno and Pete Quist (2022) at Open Secrets.org estimates that total spending on federal elections in 2022 was nearly $9 billion, about double the amount spent in 2006. They also estimate that spending in 2022 contests for state-level offices and ballot initiatives amounted to about $8 billion, $2 billion more than was spent in 2006. The top 10 individual donors in 2022 federal contests contributed $408.5 million to candidates, committees and outside election groups (Giorno 2022).

Given the importance of money in U.S. politics, it is not surprising that big donors have greater access to political leaders and significant influence over the shape of proposed legislation. Books by Martin Gilens (2012) and Larry Bartels (2017) marshal considerable statistical evidence of the disproportionate access to legislators and influence on policy proposals held by high-income individuals. In addition, Robert Erickson (2015) presents data showing that the rich are better informed about politics and much more likely to vote than citizens with lower incomes. This means that the "median voter" on economic issues, the one with the central preference regarding a particular matter, has an income level well above that of the median income household. Joseph Stiglitz (2013) and Branko Milanovic (2016) argue effectively that rising inequality has engendered elements of plutocracy in American government resulting in underinvestment in education, infrastructure and health care and little support for policies to address inequality.

The Tax Cut and Jobs Act, enacted by the Republican-controlled Congress and signed into law in late 2017, gives us an example of the way influence by the wealthy can drive public policy. This legislation made deep cuts in individual and corporate tax rates along with sweeping changes in standard and itemized deductions and many other provisions of the tax code. While the title of the bill and much of the rhetoric that surrounded its passage concerned increased job creation, the timing of the legislation was curious. Tax cuts are most often considered during recessions as a way of stimulating total spending and helping to pull the economy out of a slump. But 2017 was eight years after the end of the great recession in mid-2009 and, with the unemployment rate at 4.1% and real GDP about equal to potential GDP, it could be argued that it was a year of near full employment.

Analyses of the impact of this legislation reviewed by Gale *et al.* (2018) show that the budget deficit would increase by as much as

$2 trillion over the next decade, that real GDP would increase by less than 1% by 2027 and that the biggest tax cuts would accrue to taxpayers with the highest incomes. In 2018, it was estimated that 65% of the tax reduction would go to those in the top quintile and 20% to the top 1%. After ten years, in 2027, all of the tax cuts would go to those in the top quintile as sunset provisions written into the law are scheduled to phase out tax reductions for the lowest income groups. What was the source of political support for a major change in the tax code that generated minor economic effects and increased inequality at the expense of raising the budget deficit? I believe it was the fact that the average real disposable income of households in the top 1% of the distribution in 2017 was still 12% below their average real disposable income in 2007, just before the financial crisis and great recession.[2] This was because in 2017 income from capital gains, interest and dividends, which are important sources of income for the very rich, were well below 2007 levels. The 2017 tax cuts would substantially increase the spendable income of the richest American households.

In addition to enhancing the political power of the wealthy, rising inequality has also been cited as a factor contributing to the pronounced polarization and absence of bi-partisanship that has come to characterize the U.S. political scene in the past decade or so. Clearly, the growing gaps between the standard of living for households at the top, middle and bottom of the income distribution create a growing divergence in the economic and political interests of these groups. Inequality is also thought to contribute to polarization among lower-income households in a way that reduces their potential political power.

Payne (2017) discusses the psychological consequences of feelings of powerlessness experienced by many people in the lower reaches of an unequal income distribution. This generates a search for explanations that make conspiracy theories, racial and ethnic conflict and religious beliefs more attractive to some. The Republican party and conservative political parties in other countries have been adept at using "culture wars" to turn the focus of lower-income households away from their economic interests and to create sharp animosity between people who might join together to pursue policies designed to reduce inequality. At the same time, the Democratic party and liberal/labor parties in other countries have faced a legitimacy problem with many low-income voters because they have

---

[2] See the Congressional Budget Office data at https://www.cbo.gov/publication/57061.

turned away from the most progressive policy positions and shifted toward a more technocratic leadership (Berman 2021; McCarty 2021). One result is that we often see an expression of strong support for government action on a number of issues in public opinion polls at the same time that divided government paralyzes policymaking.

7.2.2. *Economic Consequences*

We can conclude this brief summary of various consequences from high and rising inequality with a discussion of ways in which inequality might inhibit economic growth. Here, we have to recognize that the term "economic growth" is interpreted in two ways. Economists generally refer to growth as an expansion in the productive capacity of the economy coming from an increase in the labor and capital inputs available for the production of goods and services and/or an increase in the productivity of labor and capital resulting from innovative developments of new goods and services or new productive methods. In this sense, growth refers to an increase in the ability of the economy to supply goods and services.

In more common usage in the press and general discussion, growth has a short-run connotation referring to the rate of increase of total spending or aggregate demand from one quarter or year to the next. If aggregate demand grows too slowly to keep up with the productive capacity of the economy, then some labor and capital resources will be unemployed or underemployed, a condition we call a recession. On the other hand, if aggregate demand grows too robustly and exceeds the productive capacity of the economy, the rate of price inflation will accelerate. Economists have presented evidence suggesting that a very unequal distribution of income might slow the growth of both aggregate supply and aggregate demand. I use the term "might" in the sentence above because empirical studies of the links between income inequality and supply or demand growth have come up with mixed results on the question of whether inequality has a negative effect. Still, there is enough supporting evidence for us to consider the possibility of growth consequences from high-income inequality.

To examine growth in the productive capacity of the U.S. economy, we can use the estimates of potential real GDP developed by the Congressional Budget Office (CBO) to aid in the preparation of budget forecasts and analyses of the budgetary effects of new spending and tax legislation. The CBO uses data on the available labor force, abstracting from changes due to the business cycle, and long-run trends in labor productivity to calculate potential real GDP, which gives us an estimate of the value of real goods and services that could be produced if the economy were always at full employment. Figure 7.1 plots a scatter diagram of the relationship between income inequality, measured by the Gini coefficient of household income, and the year-over-year percentage change in real potential GDP for the years from 1967 to 2021. Recall that a higher value for the Gini coefficient indicates greater inequality.

Figure 7.1 reveals a close negative correlation between annual levels of income inequality and growth in the productive capacity of the U.S. economy. The scatter plot lies near the linear trend line for all but 1967–1969 and 1997–2001. The correlation coefficient between the Gini coefficient and growth of potential GDP, even while including these two periods that might be deemed outliers, is –0.72. In the early 1970s, real potential GDP grew at an annual rate of around 3.5% while the Gini coefficient was 0.39. By the late teens and the early pandemic years, the economic growth rate had been cut in half while income inequality increased by 25%.

Of course, we know that correlation is not causation and causation might run from slowing growth to rising inequality. However, statistical

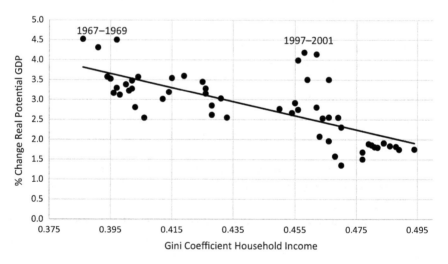

Figure 7.1:   Yearly Income Inequality and Annual Growth of Potential GDP, 1967–2021

Source: Federal Reserve Economic Data at https://fred.stlouisfed.org.

evidence for a negative causal relationship between increased inequality and slower growth is presented by Federico Cingano (2014). He studied the relationship between these variables in a sample of 30 countries over the period from 1990 to 2010. For the U.S., he finds that economic growth would have been one-fifth higher over that period if there had been no rise in income inequality.

So, what are the arguments for why an increase in inequality might be a cause of the post-1980 slowdown in the growth of U.S. productive capacity? Stiglitz (2013) points to the growing political power of high-income households as inequality increased and the resulting Republican focus on income tax rate cuts for those households since the first Reagan tax cut in 1981. He contends that those factors have combined to make it more difficult for the federal government to maintain its budgetary support for education, infrastructure and research spending, all of which have been found to increase an economy's growth potential. In particular, Stiglitz emphasizes declining federal spending on basic scientific research, which certainly played a huge role in the development of the IT industry and Silicon Valley in the 1950s. Data collected by the American Association for the Advancement of Science[3] indeed shows a substantial slowdown in the inflation-adjusted basic research budgets of federal agencies. The average annual rate of increase in real basic research budgets was 4.1% in the 1980s, 2.8% from 1990 to 2010 and 1.8% since 2010. The bipartisan support in 2022 for the CHIPS and Science Act and the Infrastructure Investment and Jobs Act, although modest, may be a sign of growing political recognition of these growth issues raised by Professor Stiglitz.

Another critical factor is the intergenerational transmission of relative income standing that we discussed above. Heather Boushey (2019) reviews evidence indicating that high inequality significantly reduces skill acquisition and mobility among children born to families in the lower percentiles of the income distribution, thereby ultimately reducing the overall level of human capital available for the production of goods and services. She also cites research indicating that entrepreneurial activity, as measured by patent holding, is significantly lower among such children. Cingano (2014) finds that a wider spread between the average level of income and the earnings of those in the four lowest deciles of the income distribution increases the effect of parental background on the acquisition

---

[3] See aaas.org/programs/r-d-budget-and-policy/historical-trends-federal-rd.

of human capital by their children. Barriers to the accumulation of skills and development of entrepreneurship interests among those born to families in the lower percentiles of an unequal distribution of income lower the skill level of the entire labor force in a way that would partially explain a negative causal effect of inequality on economic growth.

Researchers also point to an adverse economic consequence of rising inequality stemming from the potential drag on the short-term growth of total spending or aggregate demand. As a greater fraction of income accrues to high-income households, who have a lower propensity to spend and a correspondingly higher propensity to save out of their income than lower-income households, this potentially lowers the amount of total consumption spending out of a given level of income. This drag on spending growth has been given a prominent role in the literature on "secular stagnation" (Stiglitz 2013). For example, Alichi, Kantenga and Solé (2016) and Josh Bivens (2017) estimate that the increased share of income going to the highest-income households would have reduced consumer spending by 3–3.5% for each year from 1990 to 2010 in the absence of offsetting influences. These offsetting influences included Federal Reserve efforts to keep interest rates low to stimulate investment spending and an unsustainable increase in consumer debt.

Barry Cynamon and Steven Fazzari (2016) argue that the impact of inequality on the debt of lower-income households played a pivotal role in the great recession. They compare outcomes for the 5% of households earning the highest incomes with those for the remaining 95% of households at lower income levels, using an innovative method to divide aggregate consumer spending between those groups. They see three trends in the run-up to 2007, the cyclical peak before the great recession and during the downturn that followed. First, the average annual real income growth rate for the bottom 95% decelerated from 1.9% from 1960 to 1980 to 1.1% from 1980 to 2007 while growth for the top 5% increased from 2.1% to 3.9% between those periods. Second, the bottom 95% reacted to this real income slowdown by maintaining consumption and increasing their debt. The debt-to-income ratio for these households rose from 75% in 1983 to 175% in 2007. Third, when falling house prices and the 2008 financial crisis made borrowing prohibitive, consumer spending as a fraction of disposable income for the bottom 95% dropped by five percentage points, exacerbating the recession and slowing the pace of the recovery. In this situation, which involved a near-collapse of the financial system and an economic contraction that necessitated drastic monetary and fiscal policy responses, Cynamon and Fazzari (2016) make a strong case that rising inequality contributed significantly to macroeconomic instability.

The vastly disproportionate growth in the wages, wealth and income of the richest Americans relative to the rest of the population would seem to be a problem of much greater seriousness than even the serious question of basic fairness. The lasting adverse consequences of inequality for individuals and their families, the corrosive effects of inequality on the political system and the drag on the growth of total demand and potential output from inequality are all major issues. There seems to be some general agreement with this proposition from two public opinion surveys carried out in 2019. A survey of 6,878 Americans by the Pew Research Center (2020) found that 61% of all respondents agreed that "there was too much inequality in the country these days." In addition, a survey by NPR, the Robert Wood Johnson Foundation and the Chan School of Public Health at Harvard (2020) asked people from different income groups how serious of a problem were income differences between the rich and the poor. Those answering very serious or somewhat serious accounted for 75% of lower-income respondents, 70% of both middle- and higher-income respondents and 62% of respondents with incomes of $500,000 or more.

7.3. Potential Cures

A large number of policy proposals to reduce inequality have been examined in the economics literature. For example, the compendium of conference papers edited by Olivier Blanchard and Dani Rodrik (2021) offers some discussion of 25 different proposals, ranging from extending and increasing the earned income tax credit to establishing the federal government as the employer of last resort for low wage and unemployed workers. It is not my intention to review that many policy proposals here. Instead, I'll focus on those that have some chance of being enacted in the current political environment, in most cases because they would amount to changes and extensions of existing policies rather than sweeping new initiatives. While this might look like tinkering around the edges to some, the policy changes discussed in the following would have a significant impact in slowing the rate of increase and, perhaps, even reducing the levels of wage and income inequality.

7.3.1. *The Policy Environment*

There are two major factors that limit the possibility of enacting federal programs designed to reduce inequality (Bonica *et al.* 2013). The first is the political polarization between the Democratic and Republican parties that limits bipartisan support for legislation even though the two parties have an evenly shared role in governance. Political institutions like gerrymandering and the filibuster contribute to political power of the minority party. In addition, both parties rely heavily on contributions from high-income donors, who are unlikely to support legislation that would make a significant dent in the level of income inequality. In 2023, the Democrats have a slight majority in the Senate while the Republicans enjoy a slight majority in the House of Representatives. The Republican party is still committed to low taxes and a pro-business regulatory framework along with conservative positions on social issues. The Democratic party is more centrist on economic matters and liberal on social issues. Building the needed bi-partisan support for federal policy proposals addressing inequality is difficult, to say the least.

The second factor is the lack of a consensus among voters for efforts to reduce inequality. In part, this reflects the complexity of the causes of inequality and lack of knowledge about the extent to which inequality has increased (Gimpelson and Treisman 2017). In addition, there is little widespread belief among the public that high incomes are illegitimate and a focus on other issues, such as climate change, social justice, rights of women and LGBTQIA+ individuals, that distracts attention from economic issues.

This lack of consensus on inequality policy can be seen in the results of the two polls we discussed above. While 61% of the respondents to the Pew (2020) poll agreed that there was too much inequality, only 42% said reducing inequality was a top policy priority. In the NPR (2020) survey, those answering that reducing income inequality should **not** be a priority for the federal government accounted for 54% of those with top 1% incomes, 48% of those with high incomes and 43% of those with middle incomes. Only among low-income respondents was there substantial agreement (65%) that reducing inequality should be an important federal policy priority.

These polls also reveal opinions on the causes of inequality that help explain this lack of consensus and reveal the extent of political polarization on inequality policy. The Pew survey asked what contributes a great deal to inequality. Among Republican supporters, 60% said life choices while only 27% of Democratic supporters selected that option. Work effort was picked by 48% of Republicans but just 22% of Democrats. A majority of Democratic supporters (52%) said initial opportunities contributed to inequality while only 25% of Republican voters agreed. And 50% of Democrats said discrimination was a factor while just 11% of Republicans picked that option. The NPR survey asked what was important for economic success in America. Hard work was chosen by 93% of top 1% income earners, 90% of high-income persons, 89% of middle-income respondents and fully 87% of low-income people. Both polls support the idea that the American public generally believes that high incomes result largely from personal initiative and effort and therefore income disparities are not an important matter for policy. The polls also clearly highlight the differences between Republican and Democratic party supporters. With this in mind, let's consider a package of policy proposals that could be effective in reducing inequality.

A useful framework for thinking about such a policy package is presented in Figure 7.2, which we first viewed as Figure 6.7 in the previous chapter.

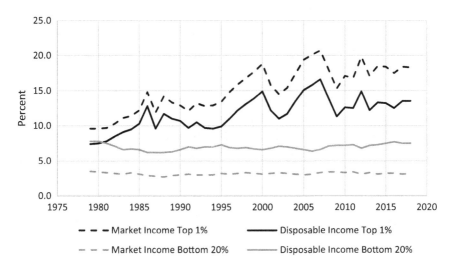

Figure 7.2:   Income Shares of the Top 1% and Bottom 20% of Households
Source: https://www.cbo.gov/publication/56575.

One way of stating the goal of policy would be to bring the disposable income shares of the top 1% and bottom 20% closer together over the next decade or two, perhaps even returning to the equality in disposable income shares seen in the first few years in the chart. One method of doing so would be to use the tax and transfer system to redistribute income, thereby shifting the disposable income share graph for the top 1% down and that for the bottom 20% up for any given share of market income. A second method would be to adopt policies that increase the market incomes of lower-income households relative to the market incomes of high-income households, thereby shrinking the gap between the market income shares of the top 1% and bottom 20%.

7.3.2. *Increasing Tax Progressivity*

A common proposal to reduce inequality is to adopt tax legislation that would make the tax system more progressive, that is, one where the share of taxes in total income rises as income rises. Thomas Piketty (2014) and many others make the case that the adoption of an income tax with a highly progressive rate structure played a significant role in the decrease of inequality from 1910 to 1950 and that reductions in the top marginal income tax rate contributed to the rise in inequality after 1980. Frank Newport (2022) reviews the results from a large number of public opinion polls on the question of whether or not the well-off pay their fair share of taxes. The majority of respondents in almost every poll he examines agrees with the proposition that upper-income households pay too little in taxes. These beliefs of opinion poll respondents are consistent with the evidence on tax incidence provided by Saez and Zucman (2020). They estimate that the total of all federal, state and local taxes was roughly 25% of income at almost all deciles of the income distribution in 2018 but dropped to 20% for the very richest households. Instead of a tax system that is progressive, this indicates a proportional tax system for low-, middle- and high-income households that becomes regressive for the highest-income earners.

Achieving a more progressive tax could be done by reversing recent tax cuts for high-income households, going from the current top bracket rate of 37% back to the 39.6% rate in 2017, changing the tax code to reduce the favorable treatment of nonlabor income and eliminating tax loopholes that make the effective tax rate on the rich much lower than the statutory rate. Also suggested by some is raising the rate and lowering the threshold for the federal inheritance tax and establishing a new wealth tax on the total value of a taxpayer's net worth. The latter changes would serve as mechanisms to reduce inequality arising from disparities in the ownership of wealth and the resulting income from wealth. I believe I have listed these changes in the order of increasing political difficulty; just reversing the 2017 tax cut would be an effective first step in addressing rising inequality but it is also one that would be very difficult to bring about in the current political environment.

The case against raising taxes on high-income households rests on the argument that doing so would slow economic growth by deterring saving, investment and innovation. While this argument is based on the marginal analysis of taxes from economic theory, in practice it is difficult to see much of an effect on economic performance. Skeptics point to the fact that U.S. economic growth was most robust during the 1950s and 1960s when the rate on the highest income bracket in the federal income tax reached 91%. We might add that Apple, Intel and Microsoft were founded in a period when the top income tax rate was 70%. A careful econometric study of this question by Owen Zidar (2019) found that U.S. employment growth was significantly enhanced by tax cuts for the bottom 90% of taxpayers but hardly affected at all by tax cuts for the top 10%.

7.3.3. *Increasing the Safety Net*

The complementary policy to raising taxes on the rich is increasing the disposable income of low-income households through enhancements to the tax and transfer system. The current impact of these factors is quite significant. In its analysis of the distribution of income, the Congressional Budget Office (2021) estimates that in 2018 the average income after taxes and transfers for households in the bottom fifth of the income distribution was 67% higher than the average income before taxes and transfers. The earned income tax credit and the child tax credit, which are fully refundable, resulted in an average federal income tax liability of –$2,700, which fully offset the effect of other federal taxes on the household budget. And means-tested transfer payments, which are available only to households whose incomes fall below a legislated threshold, boosted average household income by $15,200 for those in the lowest quintile of the income distribution. These means-tested transfers payments included health care benefits through Medicaid or the Children's Health Insurance Program (CHIP), subsidies for food purchases via the Supplemental Nutrition Assistance Program (SNAP), income transfers to the disabled and elderly from the Supplemental Security Income (SSI) program and other transfers such as housing assistance and temporary cash assistance.

In comparison with average income before taxes and transfer payments, income tax credits and means-tested payments also served to raise 2018 after-tax and transfer income for households in the 20th–40th percentile range by 6% and limited the decrease in disposable income, relative to market income before taxes and transfer payments, for the middle fifth of households to 8%. An increase in these components of the social safety net and an extension of the tax credit benefits to those not working and those without children would significantly increase the share of disposable income going to the lowest quintiles of the household income distribution.

An interesting article by Jason DeParle (2022) provides insight into what these statistics mean for the lives of low-income families. He interviewed a number of women who grew up in poor households and who live in low-income families today. The general consensus was that these federal programs plus state-level nutrition support and school lunch programs have made their children's lives much better in terms of health, housing security and opportunities for enriching activities than were their own childhoods. In addition, a pandemic-related temporary increase in the child tax credit in 2021 gives us an idea of the potential impact of expanding those benefits. A review of the data by Chuck Marr *et al.* (2022) documents how this one increase helped reduce the fraction of children living in households with below-poverty incomes by almost two-thirds. They also provide a detailed analysis of legislative changes needed to expand the coverage of the earned income tax credit and the child tax credit.

7.3.4. *Improving Labor Market Adjustment*

The research papers on the China shock to U.S. labor markets by Autor, Dorn and Hanson (2013, 2019) have attracted much attention because they demonstrate that the labor market on its own is often inefficient at redeploying workers displaced by import competition or technological change. Individuals face lengthy spells of unemployment following the loss of their jobs, eventual re-employment often involves a discount on their human capital and an increase in their likelihood of future spells of unemployment, many individuals leave the labor force entirely or work intermittently in the cash economy and their communities suffer from a decline in housing demand and retail sales and an increase in dependence on transfer payments. A program providing significant support for the training, job search and relocation of displaced workers could improve the speed with which displaced workers find reemployment and limit the steep reduction in real wages experienced currently by many when they do find new jobs.

A model would be the Trade Adjustment and Assistance for Workers Program (TAA) operated by the U.S. Department of Labor since 1974. TAA was limited to workers whose job loss was determined to be directly affected by import competition or offshoring and served relatively small numbers of displaced individuals annually with job training and extended unemployment insurance payments. Still, Benjamin Hyman (2018) finds that workers certified for TAA were more mobile between industries and locations and had greater labor force participation and higher cumulative earnings over the decade following displacement than those who were ineligible for the program. His statistical analysis indicates a causal effect of TAA participation on these labor market outcomes. An expanded TAA, to include workers displaced by automation as well as globalization and with sufficient resources to support larger numbers, would serve the bill for improving the efficiency of labor market adjustment. Unfortunately, instead of seeing this program expanded, TAA became a victim of political disputes regarding trade policy between and within the Democratic and Republican parties and was allowed to expire on July 1, 2022 (Swanson 2022).

On the demand side of distressed local labor markets, there is renewed interest in federally funded programs of place-based economic redevelopment. While economists have long argued that supporting people was more effective than subsidizing the location of businesses, the sharp decline in inter-regional migration over the last two decades, along with a corresponding end to inter-state income convergence and the emergence of regional pockets of persistently high nonemployment rates for prime age, mainly male, residents, has invigorated calls for targeting distressed areas. Austin, Glaeser and Summers (2018) develop a model that shows an overall net national gain from programs dedicated to addressing issues in specific locations as long as these programs have a bigger positive effect on job opportunities for residents of places with high rates of non-employment than residents of less-distressed areas.

Timothy Bartik (2020) reviews research on the impact of state and local place-based economic development programs that attempt to influence the location of businesses through reduced taxation, direct cash grants, tailored public investment in transportation and site improvements and government support for company-specific training. In recent years, states and localities have spent about $60 billion a year on such programs while the federal government has added $10 billion a year. There are three relevant research findings from Bartik's review. First, jobs created as a result of policy in distressed areas generate a significant number of secondary jobs, at local suppliers and at businesses responding to increased demand from rehired workers. Second, most of the new employment opportunities accrue to residents rather than in-migrants. And third, a 10% increase in policy-stimulated new jobs raises income by 4% for families in the lowest 20% of the income distribution and 1% for those in the highest 20%. Place-based policies appear to offer the possibility of reducing income inequality within and across regions if properly targeted to areas where a substantial fraction of the working-age population is out of work.

An important role for place-based economic policy can be seen in the major pieces of legislation passed during the first two years of the Biden administration. Researchers at the Brookings Institution have documented 19 place-based programs included in the American Rescue Plan, the Infrastructure Investment and Jobs Act and the CHIPS and Science Act (Muro *et al.* 2022). These have authorized $80 billion over the years to 2027 for challenge grant programs to establish new regional employment clusters in technology and energy. This major new federal initiative in the redevelopment of distressed regions envisions both incentives for job creation and training programs to supply the workers to fill those jobs. It will be interesting to see whether appropriations match authorized amounts and how this policy initiative is implemented to affect workers in localities adversely affected by globalization and technological change.

7.3.5. *Increasing the Federal Minimum Wage*

In Chapter 5, we saw that the federal minimum wage was fixed at $7.25 an hour from mid-2009 through the end of 2022. With steadily rising prices, this meant that the purchasing power of the federal minimum wage fell by 25% from the beginning of 2010 to just $5.45 at the end of 2022.

We also saw in Chapter 5 that a higher state-level minimum wage was associated with higher wages for workers at the bottom of the wage distribution relative to the median wage. States that increased their own minimum wages over the federal level the most experienced the biggest decreases in the 50–10 wage ratios over the period from 2001 to 2019. Arindrajit Dube (2019) shows that higher minimum wage levels are associated with higher incomes for low-income families. His preferred results from among a large number of alternative estimates indicate that a 10% higher minimum wage would be associated with a 3.5% higher income for families at the 10th percentile of the income distribution and a 3.3% higher income for those at the 15th percentile. Empirical results like this support the general call for increasing the federal minimum wage and indexing it to the consumer price index so that purchasing power is protected. The most recent, unsuccessful attempts to increase the federal minimum wage, the Raise the Wage Act of 2021, reintroduced in 2022, called for raising it to $15 an hour in phases ending in 2025.

Proposals to raise the minimum wage are hotly contested with opponents most often arguing that doing so would actually harm low-wage workers by reducing their employment. While that argument is supported by an application of static supply and demand analysis to the labor market, empirical studies often fail to find statistical evidence of any negative impact of the minimum wage on the number of jobs. For example, a careful recent study of state minimum wage changes over the years from 1979 to 2016 by Doruk Cengiz and colleagues (2019) found no evidence that these policy initiatives had any effect on the overall number of jobs employing low-wage workers. In a more dynamic setting, the effects of the minimum wage can be offset by reduced turnover and absenteeism, higher productivity, higher product prices and increased demand resulting from the greater earnings of workers earning the minimum wage (Ashenfelter and Jurajda 2021).

Voters seem to be less convinced than legislators by the arguments against raising the minimum wage. Since 1996, there have been 28 proposals for state minimum wage increases put to the ballot with 26 passed into law.[4] Among the states where voters favored an increase were conservative places like Arkansas, Florida, Nebraska and South Dakota. While state minimum wage laws reduce earnings inequality at the low end of wage distribution within states, they also increase inequality among

---

[4] See www.ballotpedia.org/Minimum_wage_on_the_ballot.

low-wage workers across states, so a higher federal minimum wage would have a more widespread, nationwide impact on low-wage workers. However, the failure of the 117th Congress to pass the Raise the Wage Act with a small Democratic majority in the House and control of the Senate does not augur well for an increase in the federal minimum wage in the near future.

7.3.6. *Increasing Educational Attainment*

Labor economists view human capital as the ultimate foundation for an individual's labor market potential, so educational improvements are an integral part of most inequality policy discussions. In particular, attention has been paid to the potential benefits of universal pre-kindergarten (pre-K) education and tuition-free college programs. There is substantial evidence that early childhood education programs like Head Start significantly improve participants' upward mobility as young adults (Boushey 2019). Low-cost or tuition-free education at community colleges, especially if their programs were more directly linked to the skill needs of employers as part of a distressed area redevelopment plan, has the potential to increase mid-skill wage levels. Federal spending to support increased pre-K education programs was part of two Biden administration proposals in 2021 and 2022 but was not included in the final version of the Inflation Reduction Act. As of 2022, seven states and the District of Columbia offered educational programs enrolling a majority of 4-year-old children. In addition, 20 states provided free community college education to students meeting eligibility requirements. The barrier to increased federal involvement in these programs appears to be the strong political support for local determination of educational policy. In addition, it is disturbing to see education being caught up in culture war debates leading to bans on books and political control over elementary and secondary school curricula.

There are interesting results from a recent effort to rank colleges and universities by their impact on the incomes of low-income students (Nietzel 2022). This type of ranking is based on two components. The first is an estimate of the years needed for a low-income student to recover her tuition, based on the difference in earnings from attending the college and the average earnings of a high school graduate. The second component is the proportion of low-income students, measured by Pell grant recipients, enrolled at the institution. The most highly ranked universities by this method are low-tuition regional public universities, many in California, and several historically black colleges and universities. A program that further reduced the cost of a college education at such institutions could have the effect of enhancing family investment in college education for those from low-income households and breaking the intergenerational linkage of positions in the income distribution.

7.3.7. *Enhancing Collective Bargaining*

While union membership and collective bargaining coverage are highly correlated with greater wage equality, the trend over time has seen both measures of union power fade to insignificance in the private sector of the U.S. economy. In the wake of the COVID-19 pandemic, however, there has been renewed interest in unions, as seen in increased union organizing activity, representation election victories at a number of Starbucks, Trader Joe's, Apple, Amazon and Chipotle locations, and record high levels of public support for unions in the Gallup poll (Hsu and Selyukh 2022).

The National Labor Relations Act (NLRA) gives workers the right to join unions and to bargain collectively with their employers over wages, hours and working conditions. The NLRA also proscribes certain employer and union activities as unfair labor practices. However, firms have been able to use the delays inherent in the administration of the NLRA and weak penalties for violating the law to forestall union organizing attempts and avoid negotiations for a collective bargaining agreement in cases where unions win representation rights. Over time, the shift of power to employers has been a primary determinant of the trends in union activity we noted in Chapter 5 and there are signs that the union successes of 2022 may be fleeting (Zahn 2022).

The Protecting the Right to Organize Act, passed by the House of Representatives in 2021, addressed these matters by provisions that would have streamlined representation elections, restricted some commonly used employer tactics such as captive audience speeches during organizing campaigns, and increased the penalties for employer unfair labor practices. However, the bill failed in the Senate. Suresh Naidu (2022) explains the difficulties facing union organizers in trying to forge a common worker identity in the modern workplace that would remain even if the NLRA were amended to shift some power away from employers.

In addition, he notes that the current focus of the law encourages a highly decentralized structure, with a bargaining unit at each individual Starbucks store, for example, rather than the type of centralized system found in Europe that extends union bargaining across firms, industries and regions. Reaching such a centralized system, which would greatly enhance the impact of collective bargaining on the inequality of wages, would require a complete rewrite of American labor law.

7.4. Summary

It's hard to argue with the assessment that the distributions of U.S. pay, wealth and income have moved in a way that is unfair to those not at the top percentiles. Even if we accept that monetary returns largely reflect merit and that technological change and globalization have changed the order of merit while delivering many positives to American society, it is also the case that economic and political power has been used to the benefit of the most well-off workers and families. The long-lasting negative effects of inequality and the economic forces leading to higher inequality on individuals, their families and their communities and the adverse consequences for the political system and the economy add to the call for policies to reduce the level or slow the rate of growth of inequality.

Given the extent of changes in the U.S. economy since 1980, it is somewhat surprising that inequality has not become a hotter political issue. In part, this reflects the strong meritocratic beliefs of the American populace that hard work and initiative are the prime determinants of economic success and, in part, this is due to limited information about the degree to which the distributions of pay, wealth and income have changed. Also relevant are competing political issues, such as climate change and social justice, and the stark polarization of the population largely along matters of culture, race and social affairs. While it might be tempting to prescribe the adoption of sweeping reforms designed to restore the conditions that created a much more equal U.S. economy in the years from 1950 to 1980, doing so would not be realistic in the context of the current political environment.

Instead, I have closed this little book with a list of policy proposals that would mainly involve marginal changes to existing federal economic policies. Making the tax and transfer system more progressive, providing enhanced educational and training support for young people and older workers displaced from their jobs, raising the minimum wage and index-ing it to inflation, investing in the economic development of distressed communities and making it easier for the support for unions evident in polls to translate into a stronger union movement would put a substantial dent in the growth of inequality in the future. Such policy initiatives would reinforce the coming demographic changes that promise to limit the global supply of lower-skilled workers. Populists might argue that the relevant policy list should include tough restrictions on international trade and immigration and modern-day Luddites might argue for restrictions on new technology. However, the negative effect of such policies on our standard of living would be profound.

References

Abel, Jason R., and Richard Dietz. 2020. "Women have been hit hard by the loss of routine jobs too," Federal Reserve Bank of New York *Liberty Street Economics* March 4. www.libertystreeteconomics.newyorkfed.org.

Abraham, Katharine G., John H. Haltiwanger, Kristin Sandusky, and James Spletzer. 2019. "The rise of the gig economy: Fact or fiction?" *AEA Papers and Proceedings* 109: 357–361.

Acemoglu, Daron, and Pascual Restrepo. 2018a. "The race between man and machine: Implications of technology for growth, factor shares, and employment," *American Economic Review* 108: 1488–1542.

Acemoglu, Daron, and Pascual Restrepo. 2018b. "Modeling automation," *AEA Papers and Proceedings* 108: 48–53.

Alfani, Guido. 2021. "Economic inequality in preindustrial times: Europe and beyond," *Journal of Economic Literature* 59: 3–44.

Alichi, Ali, Kory Kantenga, and Juan Solé. 2016. "Income polarization in the United States," IMF Working Paper WP/16/21. www.imf.org/en/Publications/WP/Issues/2016/12/31/Income-Polarization-in-the-United-States-44031.

Alvaredo, Fecundo, Bertrand Garbinti, and Thomas Piketty. 2017. "On the share of inheritance in aggregate wealth: Europe and the USA, 1900–2010," *Economica* 84: 239–260.

Alvaredo, Fecundo, Lucas Chancel, Thomas Piketty, Emmanuel Saez, and Gabriel Zucman. 2018b. "The elephant curve of global inequality and growth," *AEA Papers and Proceedings* 108: 103–108.

Anderson, Nick, and Danielle Douglas-Gabriel. 2021. "Colleges scramble to recruit students as nationwide enrollment plunges," *Washington Post* March 31.

Ashenfelter, Orley C., and Štěpán Jurajda. 2021. "Wages, minimum wages, and price pass-through: The case of McDonald's restaurants," *Journal of Labor Economics* 40: S179–S201.

Atalay, Enghin, Phai Phingthiengtham, Sebastian Sotelo, and Daniel Tannenbaum. 2020. "The evolution of work in the United States," *American Economic Journal: Applied Economics* 12: 1–34.

Austin, Benjamin, Edward Glaeser, and Lawrence Summers. 2018. "Jobs for the heartland: Place-based policies in 21st century America," *Brookings Papers on Economic Activity* Spring: 151–231.

Autor, David H. 2013. "The 'task approach' to labor markets: An overview," *Journal for Labour Market Research* 46: 185–199.

Autor, David H. 2015. "Why are there still so many jobs? The history and future of workplace automation," *Journal of Economic Perspectives* 29: 3–30.

Autor, David H. 2019. "Work of the past, work of the future," *AEA Papers and Proceedings* 109: 1–32.

Autor, David H., Alan Manning, and Christopher Smith. 2016. "The contribution of the minimum wage to US wage inequality over three decades: A reassessment," *AEJ: Applied Economics* 8: 58–99.

Autor, David H., Claudia Goldin, and Lawrence F. Katz. 2020. "Extending the race between education and technology," *AEA Papers and Proceedings* 110: 347–351.

Autor, David H., David Cho, Leland D. Crane, Mita Goldar, Byron Lutz, Joshua Montes, William B. Peterman, David Ratner, Daniel Villar, and Aku Yildirmaz. 2022. "The $800 billion Paycheck Protection Program: Where did the money go and why did it go there?" *Journal of Economic Perspectives* 36: 55–80.

Autor, David H., David Dorn, and Gordon H. Hanson. 2013. "The China syndrome: Local labor market effects of import competition in the United States," *American Economic Review* 103: 2121–2168.

Autor, David H., David Dorn, and Gordon H. Hanson. 2021. "On the persistence of the China Shock," NBER Working Paper 29401. www.nber.org/papers/w29401.

Azar, José, Ionna Marinescu, Marshall Steinbaum, and Bledi Taska. 2020. "Concentration in US labor markets: Evidence from online vacancy data," *Labour Economics* 66: article 101886.

Bakija, John, Adam Cole, and Bradley T. Heim. 2012. "Jobs and income growth of top earners and the causes of changing income inequality: Evidence from U.S. tax return data." www.williams.edu/Economics/wp/BakijaColeHeimJobsIncomeGrowthTopEarners.pdf.

Bartels, Larry M. 2017. *Unequal Democracy.* Princeton University Press.

Barth, Erling, Alex Bryson, James C. Davis, and Richard Freeman. 2016. "It's where you work: Increases in the dispersion of earnings across establishments and individuals in the United States," *Journal of Labor Economics* 34: S67–S97.

Bartik, Timothy J. 2020. "Using place-based jobs policies to help distressed communities," *Journal of Economic Perspectives* 34: 99–127.

Batty, Michael, Joseph Briggs, Karan Pence, Paula Smith, and Alice Volz. 2019. "The Distributional Financial Accounts," *FEDS* Notes August 30. www.federalreserve.gov/econres/notes/feds-notes/the-distributional-financial-accounts-20190830.html.

Bebchuk, Lucian, and Yaniv Grinstein. 2005. "The growth of executive pay," *Oxford Review of Economic Policy* 21: 283–303.

Bell, Alex, T.J. Hedin, Peter Mannino, Roozbeh Moghadam, Carl Romer, Geoffrey C. Schnorr, and Till von Wachter. 2022. "Estimating the disparate cumulative impact of the pandemic in administrative unemployment insurance data," *AEA Papers and Proceedings* 112: 78–84.

Benmelech, Efraim, Nittai Bergman, and Hyunseob Kim. 2022. "Strong employers and weak employees: How does employer concentration affect wages?" *Journal of Human Resources* 57: S200–S250.

Berman, Sheri. 2021. "The political conditions necessary for addressing inequality," in Blanchard, Olivier, and Dani Rodrik, editors. 2021. *Combatting Inequality*. The MIT Press. 75–84.

Bertrand, Marianne. 2020. "Gender in the twenty-first century," *AEA Papers and Proceedings* 110: 1–24.

Binder, Ariel J., and John Bound. 2019. "The declining labor market prospects of less-educated men," *Journal of Economic Perspectives* 33: 163–190.

Bivens, Josh. 2017. "Inequality is slowing US economic growth," Economic Policy Institute Report. www.epi.org/136654.

Blanchard, Olivier, and Dani Rodrik, editors. 2021. *Combatting Inequality*. The MIT Press.

Blanchet, Thomas, Emmanuel Saez, and Gabriel Zucman. 2022. "Real-time inequality," NBER Working Paper 30229. www.nber.org/papers/w30229.

Blau, Francine D., and Christopher Mackie, editors. 2017. *The Economic and Fiscal Consequences of Immigration*. The National Academies Press.

Blau, Francine D., and Lawrence M. Katz. 2017. "The gender wage gap: Extent, trends and explanations," *Journal of Economic Literature* 55: 789–865.

Bonica, Adam, Nolan McCarty, Keith T. Poole, and Howard Rosenthal. 2013. "Why hasn't democracy slowed rising inequality?" *Journal of Economic Perspectives* 27: 103–124.

Bönke, Timm, Giacomo Corneo, and Holger Lüthen. 2015. "Lifetime earnings inequality in Germany," *Journal of Labor Economics* 33: 171–207.

Borella, Margherita, Mariacristina De Nardi, and Fang Yang. 2019. "The lost ones: The opportunities and outcomes of white, non-college educated

Americans born in the 1960s," *NBER Macroeconomics Annual* 34: 67–115.

Bound, John, Breno Braga, Gaurav Khanna, and Sarah Turner. 2019. "Public Universities: The supply side of building a skilled workforce," *RSF: The Russell Sage Foundation Journal of the Social Sciences* 5: 43–66.

Bound, John, Michael F. Lovenheim, and Sarah Turner. 2010. "Why have college completion rates declined? An analysis of changing student preparation and collegiate resources," *AEJ: Applied Economics* 2: 129–157.

Boushey, Heather. 2019. *Unbound: How Inequality Constricts Our Economy and What We Can Do About It.* Harvard University Press.

Boushey, Heather, J. Bradford DeLong, and Marshall Steinbaum, editors. 2017. *After Piketty: The Agenda for Economics and Inequality.* Harvard University Press.

Boustanifar, Hamid, Everett Grant, and Ariel Reshef. 2018. "Wages and human capital in finance: International evidence, 1970–2011," *Review of Finance* 22: 699–745.

Brynjolfson, Erik, and Andrew McAfee. 2016. *The Second Machine Age.* W.W. Norton Co.

Budiman, Abby. 2020. "Key findings about U.S. immigrants," Pew Research Center, August 10. https://www.pewresearch.org/short-reads/2020/08/20/key-findings-about-u-s-immigrants/.

Card, David. 2009. "Immigration and inequality," *AEA Papers and Proceedings* 99: 1–21.

Card, David. 2022. "Who set your wage?" *American Economic Review* 112: 1075–1090.

Card, David, Thomas Lemieux, and W. Craig Riddell. 2020. "Unions and wage inequality: The roles of gender, skill and public sector employment," *Canadian Journal of Economics* 53: 148–173.

Cardoso, Matilde, Pedro Cunha Neves, Oscar Alfonso, and Elena Sochirca. 2021. "The effects of offshoring on wages: A meta-analysis," *Review of World Economics* 157: 149–179.

Case, Anne, and Angus Deaton. 2020. *Deaths of Despair and the Future of Capitalism.* Princeton University Press.

Cavenaile, Laurent. 2021. "Offshoring, computerization, labor market polarization and top income inequality," *Journal of Macroeconomics* 69: 1–19.

Cengiz, Doruk, Arindrajit Dube, Attila Lindner, and Ben Zipperer. 2019. "The effect of minimum wages on low-wage jobs," *Quarterly Journal of Economics* 134: 1405–1454.

Chetty, Raj, David Grosky, Maximilian Hell, Nathaniel Hendren, Robert Manduca, and Jimmy Narang. 2017. "The fading American dream: Trends in absolute income mobility since 1940," *Science* 356: 398–406.

Chetty, Raj, John N. Friedman, Nathaniel Hendren, and Michael Stepner. 2020. "How did Covid-19 and stabilization policies affect spending and employment? A new real-time economic tracker based on private sector data," NBER Working Paper 27431. www.nber.org/papers/w27341.

Chetty, Raj, Nathaniel Hendren, Patrick Kline, Emmanuel Saez, and Nicholas Turner. 2014. "Is the United States still a land of opportunity? Recent trends in intergenerational mobility," *AEA Papers and Proceedings* 104: 141–147.

Chetverikov, Denis, Bradley Larsen, and Christopher Palmer. 2016. "IV quantile regression for group-level treatments, with an application to the distributional effects of trade," *Econometrica* 84: 809–833.

Cingano, Federico. 2014. "Trends in income inequality and its impact on economic growth," OECD Social, Employment and Migration Working Papers No. 163. www.oecd-ilibrary.org/social-issues-migration-health/ trends-in-income-inequality-and-its-impact-on-economic-growth_ 5jxrjncwxv6j-en.

Cohen, Adam. 2020. *Supreme Inequality: The Supreme Court's Fifty-Year Battle for a More Unjust America.* Penguin Press.

Congressional Budget Office. 2021. *The Distribution of Household Income, 2018.* www.cbo.gov/publication/57061.

Cortes, Guido Matias. 2016. "Where have the middle-wage workers gone? A study of polarization using panel data," *Journal of Labor Economics* 34: 63–105.

Cynamon, Barry Z., and Steven M. Fazzari. 2016. "Inequality, the great recession and slow recovery," *Cambridge Journal of Economics* 40: 373–399.

Daly, Mary C., Bart Hobijn, and Joseph H. Pedtke. 2017. "Disappointing facts about the black-white wage gap," Federal Reserve Bank of San Francisco *Economic Letter* September: 5.

Davis, Jonathan, and Bhashkar Mazumder. 2017. "The decline in intergenerational mobility after 1980," Federal Reserve Bank of Chicago Working Paper No. 2017-05. www.chicagofed.org/publications/working-papers/2017/ wp2017-05.

DeParle, Jason. 2022. "How poverty programs aided children from one generation to the next," *New York Times* September 12.

Derenoncourt, Ellora, Chi Hyun Kim, Moritz Kuhn, and Moritz Schularick. 2022. "Wealth of two nations: The U.S. racial wealth gap, 1860–2020," NBER Working Paper 30101. www.nber.org/papers.w30101.

Dube, Arindrajit. 2019. "Minimum wages and the distribution of family incomes," *American Economic Journal: Applied Economics* 11: 268–304.

Dube, Arindrajit, and Ethan Kaplan. 2010. "Does outsourcing reduce wages in the low-wage service occupations? Evidence from janitors and guards," *Industrial and Labor Relations Review* 63: 287–306.

Erikson, Robert S. 2015. "Income inequality and policy responsiveness," *Annual Review of Political Science* 18: 11–19.

Fagereng, Andreas, Luigi Guiso, Davide Malacrino, and Luigi Pistaferri. 2020. "Heterogeneity and persistence in returns to wealth," *Econometrica* 88: 115–170.

Farber, Henry, and Bruce Western. 2001. "Accounting for the decline in unions in the private sector, 1973–1998," *Journal of Labor Research* 22: 459–485.

Farber, Henry S., Daniel Herbst, and Ilyana Kuziemko. 2021. "Unions and inequality over the twentieth century: New evidence from survey data," *Quarterly Journal of Economics* 136: 1325–1385.

Farrell, Diana, Susan Lund, Oskar Skau, Charles Atkins, Jan Philipp Mengeringhaus, and Moira S. Pierce. 2008. *Mapping Global Capital Markets: Fifth Annual Report*. McKinsey Global Institute. https://www.mckinsey.com/~/media/mckinsey/featured%20insights/global%20capital%20markets/mapping%20global%20capital%20markets%20fifth%20annual%20report/mgi_mapping_capital_markets_fifth_annual_report.pdf.

Feiveson, Laura, and John Sabelhaus. 2018. "How does intergenerational wealth transmission affect wealth concentration?" *FEDS* Notes. www.federalreserve.gov/econres/notes/feds-notes/how-does-intergenerational-wealth-transmission-affect-wealth-concentration-20180601.html.

Fiorito, Jack. 2007. "The state of unions in the United States," *Journal of Labor Research* 28: 44–68.

Foote, Christopher L., and Richard W. Ryan. 2014. "Labor-market polarization over the business cycle," *NBER Macroeconomics Annual* 29: 371–413.

Fortin, Nicole M., Thomas Lemieux, and Neil Lloyd. 2021. "Labor market institutions and the distribution of wages: The role of spillover effects," *Journal of Labor Economics* 39: S369–S412.

Gaggl, Paul, and Sylvia Kaufmann. 2020. "The cyclical component of labor market polarization and jobless recoveries in the US," *Journal of Monetary Economics* 116: 334–347.

Galbraith, John Kenneth. 1967. *The New Industrial State*. Houghton Mifflin.

Gale, William G., Hilary Gelfond, Aaron Krupkin, Mark J. Mazur, and Eric Toder. 2018. *Effects of the Tax Cuts and Jobs Act: A Preliminary Analysis*. Tax Policy Center. www.taxpolicycenter.org/sites/default/files/publication/155349/2018.06.08_tcja_summary_paper_final_0.pdf.

Garnero, Andrea, Alexander Hijzen, and Sébastien Martin. 2019. "More unequal, but more mobile? Earnings inequality and mobility in OECD countries," *Labour Economics* 56: 26–35.

Giandrea, Michael D., and Shawn Sprague. 2017. "Estimating the U.S. labor share," *Monthly Labor Review* February.

Gilens, Martin. 2012. *Affluence and Influence*. Princeton University Press.

Gimpelson, Vladimir, and Daniel Treisman. 2017. "Misperceiving inequality," *Economics and Politics* 30: 27–54.

Giorno, Taylor. 2022. "2022 federal midterm election spending to top $9.3 billion," Open Secrets *News* September 26. www.opensecrets.org/news/2022/09/2022-midterm-election-spending-on-track-to-top-9-3-billion/.

Giorno, Taylor, and Pete Quist. 2022. "Total cost of 2022 state and federal elections projected to exceed $16.7 billion," Open Secrets *News* November 3. www.opensecrets.org/news/2022/11/total-cost-of-2022-state-and-federal-elections-projected-to-exceed-16-7-billion/.

Godard, John. 2009. "The exceptional decline of the American labor movement," *Industrial and Labor Relations Review* 63: 82–108.

Goldin, Claudia, and Lawrence F. Katz. 2008. *The Race between Education and Technology.* The Belknap Press of Harvard University Press.

Goldschmidt, Deborah, and Johannes F. Schmieder. 2017. "The rise of domestic outsourcing and the evolution of the German wage structure," *Quarterly Journal of Economics* 132: 1165–1217.

Goodhart, Charles, and Manoj Pradhan. 2020. *The Great Demographic Reversal.* Palgrave Macmillan.

Gould, Eric D. 2018. "Explaining the unexplained: Residual wage inequality, manufacturing decline and low-skilled immigration," *Economic Journal* 129: 1281–1326.

Greenwood, Jeremy, Nezih Guner, George Kocharkov, and Cezar Santos. 2014. "Marry your like: Assortative mating and income inequality," *AEA Papers and Proceedings* 104: 348–353.

Haltiwanger, John C., Henry R. Hyatt, and James Spletzer. 2022. "Industries, mega firms and increasing inequality," NBER Working Paper 29920. www.nber.org/papers/w29920.

Handwerker, Elizabeth Weber, and James R. Spletzer. 2016. "The role of establishments and the concentration of occupations in wage inequality," *Research in Labor Economics* 43: 167–193.

Helpman, Elhanan. 2018. *Globalization and Inequality.* Harvard University Press.

Hershbein, Brad, Melissa S. Kearney, and Luke W. Pardue. 2020. "College attainment, income inequality, and economic security: A simulation exercise," *AEA Papers and Proceedings* 110: 352–355.

Hirsch, Barry T., and David A. McPherson. 2003. "Union membership and coverage database from the Current Population Survey: Note," *Industrial and Labor Relations Review* 56: 349–354.

Hoffmann, Florian, David S. Lee, and Thomas Lemieux. 2020. "Growing income inequality in the United States and other advanced economies," *Journal of Economic Perspective* 34: 52–78.

Hoxby, Caroline M. 2009. "The changing selectivity of American colleges," *Journal of Economic Perspectives* 23: 95–118.

Hsu, Andrea, and Alina Selyukh. 2022. "Union wins made big news this year. Here are 5 reasons why it's not the full story," *NPR* December 27. https://www.npr.org/2022/12/27/1145090566/labor-unions-organizing-elections-worker-rights-wages.

Hummels, David, Jakob R. Munch, and Chong Xiang. 2018. "Offshoring and the labor market," *Journal of Economic Literature* 56: 981–1028.

Humpage, Owen F., and Nicholas V. Karamouzis. 1985. "The dollar in the eighties," Federal Reserve Bank of Cleveland *Economic Commentary* September. www.clevelandfed.org/publications/economic-commentary/1985/ec-1985 0901-the-dollar-in-the-eighties.

Hyclak, Thomas. 1979. "The effect of unions on earnings inequality in local labor markets," *Industrial and Labor Relations Review* 33: 77–84.

Hyman, Benjamin C. 2018. "Can displaced labor be retrained? Evidence from quasi-random assignment to Trade Adjustment Assistance," *Proceedings, Annual Conference on Taxation and Minutes of the Annual Meeting of the National Tax Association* 111: 1–70.

Jaimovich, Nir, and Henry E. Siu. 2020. "Job polarization and jobless recoveries," *Review of Economics and Statistics* 102: 129–147.

James, Harold. 2021. "Globalization's coming golden age: Why crisis ends in connection," *Foreign Affairs* May/June.

Jäntti, Markus, and Stephen P. Jenkins. 2015. "Income mobility," *Handbook of Income Distribution*, 2: 807–935.

Joe, Dong-Hee, and Seongman Moon. 2020. "Minimum wages and wage inequality in the OECD countries," *East Asian Economic Review* 24: 253–273.

Kaplan, Stephen N., and Joshua Rauh. 2013. "It's the market: The broad-based rise in the return to top talent," *Journal of Economic Perspectives* 27: 35–56.

Katz, Lawrence F., and Alan B. Krueger. 2019. "Understanding trends in alternative work arrangements in the United States," *RSF: The Russell Sage Foundation Journal of the Social Sciences* 5: 132–146.

Kaufman, Bruce E. 2001. "The theory and practice of strategic HRM and participative management: Antecedents in early industrial relations," *Human Resource Management Review* 11: 505–533.

Kletzer, Lori G. 1998. "Job displacement," *Journal of Economic Perspectives* 12: 115–136.

Kopczuk, Wojciech, and Eric Zwik. 2020. "Business incomes at the top," *Journal of Economic Perspectives* 34: 27–51.

Kopczuk, Wojciech, Emmanuel Saez, and Jae Song. 2010. "Earnings inequality and mobility in the United States: Evidence from Social Security data since 1937," *Quarterly Journal of Economics* 125: 91–128.

Kristal, Tali, and Yinon Cohen. 2016. "The causes of rising wage inequality: The race between institutions and technology," *Socio-Economic Review* 14: 1–26.

Krueger, Alan B. 2018. "Luncheon Address: Reflections on dwindling worker bargaining power and monetary policy," https://www.kansascityfed.org/Jackson%20Hole/documents/6984/Lunch_JH2018.pdf.

Kuhn, Moritz, Moritz Schularick, and Ulrike I. Steins. 2020. "Income and wealth inequality in America, 1949–2016," *Journal of Political Economy* 128: 3469–3519.

Lachowska, Marta, Alexandre Mas, and Stephen Woodbury. 2020. "Sources of displaced workers' long-term earnings losses," *American Economic Review* 110: 3231–3266.

Lakner, Christoph, and Branko Milanovic. 2016. "Global income distribution: From the fall of the Berlin Wall to the Great Recession," *The World Bank Economic Review* 30: 203–232.

Lamadon, Thibaut, Magne Mostad, and Bradley Setzler. 2022. "Imperfect competition, compensating differentials and rent sharing in the U.S. labor market," *American Economic Review* 112: 169–212.

Lee, Chul-In, and Gary Solon. 2009. "Trends in intergenerational income mobility," *Review of Economics and Statistics* 91: 766–772.

Lee, Eunhee. 2020. "Trade, inequality, and the endogenous sorting of heterogeneous workers," *Journal of International Economics* 125: 1–22.

Levine, Phillip B., Jennifer Ma, and Lauren C. Russell. 2020. "Do college applicants respond to changes in sticker prices even when they don't matter?" NBER Working Paper 26910. www.nber.org/papers/w26910.

Lindert, Peter H., and Jeffery G. Williamson. 2016. *Unequal Gains: American Growth and Inequality since 1700.* Princeton University Press.

Mankiw, N. Gregory. 2015. "Yes, r>g. So what?" *AEA Papers and Proceedings* 105: 43–47.

Manning, Alan. 2021. "Monopsony in labor markets: A review," *ILR Review* 74: 3–26.

Marr, Chuck, Kris Cox, Sarah Calame, Stephanie Hingtgen, George Fenton, and Arloc Sherman. 2022. "Year-end tax policy priority: Expand the Child Tax Credit for the 19 million children who receive less than the full credit," Center on Budget and Policy Priorities, November 15. https://www.cbpp.org/research/federal-tax/year-end-tax-policy-priority-expand-the-child-tax-credit-for-the-19-million.

Mazumder, Bhaskhar. 2005. "Fortunate sons: New estimates of intergenerational mobility in the United States using Social Security earnings data," *Review of Economics and Statistics* 87: 235–255.

McCarty, Nolan. 2021. "The political obstacles to tackling economic inequality," in Blanchard, Olivier, and Dani Rodrik, editors. 2021. *Combatting Inequality.* The MIT Press. 85–90.

Mervosh, Sarah. 2022. "The pandemic erased two decades of progress in math and reading," *New York Times* September 1.

Milanovic, Branko. 2016. *Global Inequality.* The Belknap Press of Harvard University Press.

Mishel, Lawrence, and Jori Kandra. 2020. "CEO compensation surged 14% in 2019 to $21.3 million," Economic Policy Institute Report. www.epi.org/204513.

Mitchell, Michael, Michael Leachman, and Matt Saenz. 2019. "State higher education funding cuts have pushed costs to students, worsened inequality," Center on Budget and Policy Priorities, October 24. www.cbpp.org/blog/state-higher-education-cuts-pushed-costs-to-students-worsened-inequality.

Muro, Mark, Robert Maxim, Joseph Parilla, and Xavier de Souiza Briggs. 2022. "Breaking down an $80 billion surge in place-based industrial policy," *The Avenue* December 15. www.brookings.edu/blog/the-avenue/.

Naidu, Suresh. 2022. "Is there any future for a US labor movement?" *Journal of Economic Perspectives* 36: 3–28.

Newport, Frank. 2022. "Average American remains OK with higher taxes on rich," *Polling Matters* August 12. www.news.gallup.com/opinion/polling-matters/396737/average-american-remains-higher-taxes-rich.aspx.

Nietzel, Michael T. 2022. "New study shows which colleges help low-income students get ahead," *Forbes* January 27.

NPR, the Robert Wood Johnson Foundation, and Harvard T. H. Chan School of Public Health. 2020. "Life experiences and income inequality in the United States." https://www.rwjf.org/en/insights/our-research/2019/12/life-experiences-and-income-inequality-in-the-united-states.html.

Payne, Keith. 2017. *The Broken Ladder.* Penguin Books.

Pew Research Center. 2020. "Most Americans say there is too much inequality in the U.S., but fewer than half call it a top priority." https://www.pewresearch.org/social-trends/wp-content/uploads/sites/3/2020/01/PSDT_01.09.20_economic-inequailty_FULL.pdf.

Phalippou, Ludovic. 2020. "An inconvenient fact: Private Equity returns and the billionaire factory," *The Journal of Investing* 30: 11–39.

Philippon, Thomas, and Ariell Reshef. 2012. "Wages and human capital in the US finance industry: 1909–2006," *Quarterly Journal of Economics* 127: 1551–1609.

Piketty, Thomas. 2014. *Capital in the Twenty-First Century.* The Belknap Press of Harvard University Press.

Rosen, Sherwin. 1981. "The economics of superstars," *American Economic Review* 71: 845–858.

Saez, Emmanuel, and Gabriel Zucman. 2020. "The rise of income and wealth inequality in America: Evidence from distributional macroeconomic accounts," *Journal of Economic Perspectives* 34: 3–26.

Schumpeter, Joseph. 1942. *Capitalism, Socialism and Democracy*, Third Edition. Harper & Row.

Shih, Willy C. 2020. "Global supply chains in a post-pandemic world," *Harvard Business Review* September–October.

Smith, Adam. 1937. *The Wealth of Nations*, The Modern Library Edition.

Sokalova, Anna, and Todd Sorensen. 2021. "Monopsony in labor markets: A meta-analysis," *ILR Review* 74: 27–55.

Solon, Gary. 2018. "What do we know so far about multigenerational mobility?" *Economic Journal* 128: F340–F352.

Spencer, Aron, and Bruce A. Kirchhoff. 2006. "Schumpeter and new technology based firms: Towards a framework for how NTBFs cause creative destruction," *International Entrepreneurship Management Journal* 2: 145–156.

Stansbury, Anna, and Lawrence H. Summers. 2020. "The declining worker power hypothesis: An explanation for the recent evolution of the American economy," *Brookings Papers on Economic Activity* Spring: 1–96.

Steinberg, Joseph B. 2019. "On the source of U.S. trade deficits: Global savings glut or domestic saving drought?" *Review of Economic Dynamics* 31: 200–223.

Stiglitz, Joseph E. 2013. *The Price of Inequality*. W.W. Norton & Co.

Stolper, Wolfgang, and Paul A. Samuelson. 1941. "Protection and real wages," *Review of Economic Studies* 9: 58–73.

Swanson, Ana. 2022. "America's safety net for workers hurt by globalization is falling apart," *New York Times* July 20.

Tan, Annabel X., Jessica A. Hinman, and Hoda S. Abdel Magid. 2021. "Association between income inequality and county level Covid-19 cases and deaths in the US," *JAMA Network Open.* doi:10.1001/jamanetwork open.2021.8799.

Taylor, Lance, and Özlem Ömer. 2020. *Macroeconomic Inequality from Reagan to Trump.* Cambridge University Press.

Timmer, Marcel P., Abdul Azeez Erumban, Bart Los, Robert Stehrer, and Gaaitzen J. de Vries. 2014. "Slicing up global value chains," *Journal of Economic Perspectives* 28: 99–118.

Toney, Jermaine, and Cassandra L. Robertson. 2021. "Intergenerational economic mobility and the racial wealth gap," *AEA Papers and Proceedings* 111: 206–210.

Tyson, Laura, and Michael Spence. 2017. "Exploring the effects of technology on income and wealth inequality," in Boushey, Heather, J. Bradford DeLong, and Marshall Steinbaum, editors. 2017. *After Piketty: The Agenda for Economics and Inequality.* Harvard University Press 170–208.

U.S. Government Accountability Office. 2019. "Retirement security: Income and wealth disparities continue through old age," Report to Ranking Member, Committee on the Budget, U.S. Senate, GAO-19-587. www.gao.gov/assets/gao-19-587.pdf.

Webber, Douglas. 2015. "Firm market power and the earnings distribution," *Labour Economics* 35: 123–134.

Weil, David. 2014. *The Fissured Workplace.* Harvard University Press.

Wood, Adrian. 2018. "The 1990s trade and wages debate in retrospect," *World Economy* 41: 975–999.

Xavier, Inês. 2021. "Wealth inequality in the U.S.: The role of heterogeneous returns." https://ssrn.com/abstract=3915439.

Zahn, Max. 2022. "Amazon and Starbucks workers led a union resurgence in 2022. Will it last?" *ABC News* December 22. www.abcnews.go.com/business/amazon-starbucks-workers-led-union-resurgence-2022/story?id=95090198.

Zidar, Owen. 2019. "Tax cuts for whom? Heterogeneous effects of income tax changes on growth and employment," *Journal of Political Economy* 127: 1437–1472.

Index

Printed in the United States
by Baker & Taylor Publisher Services